How To Care F

Everything You Need To Know To Start Beekeeping And Confidently Care For Your Bees

Introduction

Does the thought of having unlimited access to pure and delicious honey and pollination agents in your home appeal to you?

Would you like an extensive guide that illustrates the ins and outs of keeping bees at home?

If you've answered YES, then you've come to the right place.

With so many things to learn about beekeeping, it is very easy for beginners with no proper guidance to make many mistakes that might be costly. Any bee keeper will tell you that working with bees is a challenge, partly because bees are dangerous, and harvesting their honey is not as easy as it may seem.

Fortunately, the good thing about bees is that they practically take care of themselves. Unlike most domestic animals that require consistent upkeep and looking, for example, sheep, chicken, cows, or goats that require, bees are independent creatures. They clean themselves, forage for their food and water, and even make an effort to store your harvest for you. That means rearing bees requires very minimal input but offers great rewards of pure honey and pollination for your crops.

Do you love the idea of keeping bees at home, but the fear of bee stings and not knowing how to go about keeping bees keeps holding you back?

If you can relate to that, do not worry. This elaborate guide will teach you everything you need to know about raising bees so that you can reap the immense benefits.

Before we jump in:

The Great Bee Crisis

In the last 15 years or so, bee colonies have been slowly disappearing in what many experts call the colony collapse disorder. And yet, as these numbers continue dwindling slowly, honey bees are one of the most important agricultural commodities in any country. Worldwide, honey bees and other agents of pollination produce about $170 billion in crops.

Therefore, there is a need to mitigate the effects of the dwindling number of honey bees before we experience problems in crop management and production.

One way to do this is by increasing the number of professional and DIY beekeepers worldwide, which this book intends to show you.

Now that you have committed to being a keeper, the first thing we shall look at is how this benefits you and what you stand to gain the most from it.

Table of Content

Introduction _____ 2

   The Great Bee Crisis_____ 3

Chapter 1 _____ 10

Bee Keeping 101 _____ 10

The WHYs of Being a Beekeeper _____ 11

   The 10 Standout Benefits of Beekeeping _____ 11

The Challenges of Beekeeping _____ 18

   Beekeeping Laws By State _____ 26

The Cost of Beekeeping _____ 33

   Beekeeping Tools _____ 34

   Beehive Configuration _____ 35

   Cost of bees _____ 37

   Time cost _____ 39

   Animal protection _____ 39

   Winterization _____ 40

   Miscellaneous Costs _____ 41

   How to Save on Beekeeping _____ 41

Other Beekeeping Considerations _____ 43

Chapter 2 _____ 45

Bee Hierarchy & The Hive _____ 45

The Queen _____ 48

Workers _____ 52

    Laying Workers _____ 53

    Drone Bees _____ 54

Bee Development Stages _____ 56

    The Bee Cycle _____ 57

    Seasonal Cycles of Activities in Colonies _____ 60

Chapter 3 _____ 66

A Home For Your Bees _____ 66

    The Modern Commercial Beekeeper _____ 67

    The Treatment-free Beekeeper _____ 68

    The Chemical-free Beekeeper Who Treats _____ 70

    What Is A Beehive? _____ 72

    The Most Common Beehive Configurations _____ 73

How to Build Your Beehive _____ 87

Chapter 4 94

The Right Bees For You 94

    The Most Common Bee Species 95

    Italian Bees 96

    Carnolians 97

    Buckfast bees 98

    Hybrid bees 99

    Other Species 100

How to Choose The Best Location For Your Bees 101

Where to Get Bees 106

    1: Package bees 106

    2: Nucleus hive 107

    Getting Bees in The Wild 107

    The Best Time To Get Your Bees 109

    Number of Bees Required to Start a Hive .. 109

Bringing The Bees Home 111

    How Packaged Bees Travel 111

    Preparing for the Bees 112

    Putting the Bees into the Beehive _____ 113

Chapter 5 _____ 115

Checking and Maintaining Your Bees _____ 115

    When Not to Open a Beehive _____ 118

    What You Need for a Hive Inspection _____ 118

    Routine Hive Inspection Procedure _____ 120

    Record Keeping for Beekeepers _____ 123

    Importance of Bee Keeping Records _____ 123

    How to Deal with a Bee Sting _____ 131

    Home Remedies For A Bee Sting _____ 132

Chapter 6 _____ 135

Bees Throughout The Seasons _____ 135

    Spring _____ 136

    Winter _____ 137

    Autumn _____ 138

    Summer _____ 139

Chapter 7 _____ 140

All About Honey _____ 140

What is Honey? _____ 141

How Honey Gets its Flavor, Color, and Fragrance _____ 142

How Many Bees Does It Take To Make Honey? 143

How Often Can You Harvest Your Honey? ___ 143

Honey Harvesting Equipment _____ 144

How to Extract Honey From The Hive_____ 150

How to Extract the Honey _____ 153

Benefits of Honey and Honeycomb _____ 154

Chapter 8 _____ 157

Healthy Bees and Productive Colony _____ 157

Signs of a Healthy Hive_____ 158

Bees Absconding _____ 170

Conclusion _____ 173

Chapter 1

Bee Keeping 101

The WHYs of Being a Beekeeper

Before you can go ahead and begin the process of beekeeping, there are several things you need to have in mind.

The first is that it's important to know the benefits you stand to gain from being a bee farmer, the legality of beekeeping in your area, the challenges you expect, and all other important things to consider. Having this as your first stop is especially important because it allows you to prepare yourself for the task ahead.

Bees are very beneficial. Let's focus on the benefits of beekeeping:

The 10 Standout Benefits of Beekeeping

When most people think about bees, they only think that bees are only useful for their honey. However, bees offer so many benefits not only to you but to the environment as a whole.

Here is a list of the many benefits you stand to gain from beekeeping so that you can discover your WHY for having the passion for being a beekeeper:

#: Helps in conserving the environment

Bees are some of the best global pollinators; they transfer pollen from one plant to another, which is especially critical to growing food and agriculture, which accounts for 30% of the world's food production.

In addition, bees are necessary for wild plants because estimates show that more than 90% of all the plants in the wild rely on pollinators to thrive and survive. This means that without bees, most plants would just die.

Also, bees don't just benefit the environment around them; they can gather pollen and nectar from miles around while spreading sustainability and diversity throughout the ecosystem.

#: Helps in pollinating crops and flowers

For any crop to be productive, it has to receive pollen from any agent of pollination. And since bees are the primary agents of pollination, they are a critical part of ensuring that many plants reproduce and thrive. Therefore, if you're looking to have a bountiful harvest, add some bees to your garden!

If you didn't know, one bee hive is enough to increase how many flowers bloom and flourish in a garden. So in one way, bees help beautify a place as they offer food security to those around them.

#: *They don't consume a lot of space*

Unlike most domestic animals, bees consume minimal space. Most beehives are no more than 20 inches by 16 inches, and therefore, they can't take up more than a few square feet of your land.

Moreover, bees don't mind wherever you decide to keep them. Whether it is on a tree, a farm, in the suburbs, or even if you want to keep them on the roof, bees could care less. So, you don't have to worry about having a huge space when it comes to keeping bees in your home.

#: *Minimal input required*

As mentioned earlier, bees are one of the most independent creatures one can keep. Therefore, just about anyone can make bees work; even if you have a full-time job, you can keep bees.

In addition, bees don't require much maintenance, just about 30 minutes each week and a little extra time each year to collect honey. Also, the bees practically clean themselves, feed themselves, and even harvest the produce all in one place for you.

Therefore, this means anybody willing to keep bees can easily do so. Finally, there is nothing as marvelous as the taste and smell of fresh honey, and any novice beekeeper can produce honey as easily as someone with years of experience.

#: *Honey has health benefits*

The properties found in honey have made it the perfect remedy for various illnesses for as long as man has existed.

Most people claim that honey is excellent for treating a sore throat, boosting memory, killing antibiotic-resistant bacteria, healing wounds, preventing an unhealthy reduction in white blood cells, and fixing dandruff as well as scalp issues. Some people also claim that honey can help build immunity to allergies through exposure.

Although not all of these claims about honey are backed by science, honey has shown great results in dealing with most health concerns. It even provides a healthier option to refined sugar and is full of beneficial nutrients.

Also, honey doesn't spoil under most circumstances and can last for ages.

#: *Produces many beneficial products*

Beekeeping is one of those many ideas that pay you back all your expenditure and some more. When you think about the products you'll get from beekeeping, honey is probably the first thing. However, beekeeping produces many other lucrative products such as beeswax, propolis, pollen, royal jelly, and honeycomb.

Some of these products are very useful for medicinal purposes and food products, while many others act as raw materials for other things.

For example, propolis has proven itself a helpful way to deal with allergies, dermatological, oral, and gastrointestinal problems. On the other hand, royal jelly is good for wound healing, reproductive health, neurodegenerative effects, and aging, to mention just some of its many other uses.

#: *It is very economical*

Unlike most of the hobbies you can do, beekeeping is one of the least costly. If you set things up correctly, it can pay for itself or earn you extra money without emptying your wallets.

Imagine getting your first beehive, including the bees, clothing, and equipment for no more than $500, and how much you can reap from that over time.

Also, the maintenance cost is almost zero because bees practically take care of themselves. Therefore, you can easily get into beekeeping with a low budget making it very economical.

#: It is therapeutic

Beekeeping is both a hobby and a business opportunity. And like many hobbies, beekeeping allows you to relax as you connect with nature. Many beekeepers have even confirmed this claim by stating that beekeeping helps reduce stress.

You might think that dealing with these harmful creatures cannot in any way be soothing, but that's not the case. Instead, being with your bees, tending to them, and taking care of them can help you forget your problems of the day as you feel at peace with nature.

#: It helps the economy

As discussed earlier, bees can help increase yields and the growth of vegetation around a place. That includes everything from berries to apples to vegetables like cucumber. In America, this translates to over $15 billion worth of crops.

Besides that, the honey that the bees produce in the US alone has an approximate valuation of over $150 million. That means that the more bees people keep, the higher the chances of reduced food cost, because as you know, thanks to the pollination of fruits and vegetables, a bountiful harvest motivates growth within a country.

#: *To save the bee crisis*

At the beginning of this book, we talked about the dwindling numbers of bees worldwide, a trend that many environmental experts find worrying. And so, beekeeping is a chance to become part of the solution because when you keep bees, the numbers start to rise steadily.

Without watering down these and the many other benefits of keeping bees, bee hives usually face many challenges during the year. And so, as a beekeeper, you have to do everything in your power to make sure they survive. In addition, as a beekeeper, you have to become more aware of the way bees live, and therefore you'll be part of the group creating awareness surrounding beekeeping.

We've just mentioned a few of the many benefits you stand to gain from beekeeping. However, like most things, beekeeping has its downfalls, something we shall focus on in the next chapter:

The Challenges of Beekeeping

While none of us can deny that beekeeping has its benefits, there is also a downside to it all. There are some likely challenges and problems you're going to face along the journey, especially if you're completely new to beekeeping.

The most standout of these challenges are:

#: Bees can be dangerous

Although bees are quite productive in producing honey, they can also be quite dangerous to keep because of bee stings. Anyone with firsthand experience with a bee sting can tell you that it is quite painful and very unsettling. Furthermore, if you happen to be allergic to bee stings, you can even die if you don't receive medical care quickly. Therefore, this poses a challenge to beekeepers, especially if you're a beginner because you're not well acquainted with the whole process.

It is advisable to seek professional advice if you're a beginner; that way, you will also determine if you're allergic to bee stings. Also, learning to manage the hives properly can help lessen the stinging episodes.

#: Bee diseases

As we had previously discussed, bee populations have been in decline for the past few decades. Some of the most common issues causing this are pesticides, diseases, and parasites. However, sometimes there is just no explanation for an unhealthy hive. This poses a challenge, especially to beginners, because you might end up with an extremely reduced bee population if you don't know how to manage your hive.

It's, therefore, important to take time to learn how to keep your bees healthy and investigate the problems facing other beekeepers in your area. That way, you can prepare well in advance for arising contingencies.

#: Cost of supplies

Because bees are low maintenance because they practically take care of themselves, the initial cost might be quite intimidating for new beekeepers. That is because you'll have to purchase such things like protective clothing, a bee hive, a smoker, among other things. This can be challenging, especially for beginners, because it can be quite challenging to get started without enough startup capital.

Therefore, make sure to survey the best deals for combined supplies, or you can decide to reduce the cost by building a hive at home. But above all, make sure you have some money saved up for startup capital.

#: Lower prioritization of beekeeping

Compared to other enterprises in the wider Agricultural sector, beekeeping often has the lowest prioritization. For most people that consider investing or getting into agriculture, beekeeping is usually the last in their list of options.

This can be problematic because when beekeeping is not a priority, it usually gets the least or no funding. When it comes to funding coming from the government, beekeeping usually gets inadequate funding, making it difficult for the industry to grow and expand.

#: Underdeveloped marketing system

When it comes to selling hive products locally and internationally, beekeeping ranks the least in the agricultural sector. Whether it is due to poor quality or inadequate marketing organization, there is a real marketing challenge in this segment.

This often leads to poor product packaging and marketing of bee products at a throwaway price, making it difficult to make any profits. As a beginner beekeeper, that is a problem because you might make a bad investment if the market disfavors you.

There is, therefore, a need to strengthen the marketing system if beekeeping is to grow and become lucrative.

#: Inadequate training

Another challenge facing most beekeepers is the lack of proper guidance. And like any other activity, you need the right guidance and appropriate skills to execute beekeeping properly. Without proper training, there is an increased risk of making mistakes, some of which might be costly. This is especially true when it comes to hive management and marketing strategies for it to become lucrative.

As a beginner beekeeper, if you don't get proper guidance, your chances of success are very low. Therefore, to avoid problems in the future, make sure you get proper guidance as you'll get from this elaborate guide.

#: Inadequate research and equipment

Another critical issue facing the beekeeping industry is the unavailability of proper beekeeping equipment for most beekeepers. Most beekeepers only have access to limited equipment, making it difficult to become a beekeeper.

Without the proper equipment or gear, you can't manage your hives properly, especially because bees are dangerous. But, unfortunately, most governments are doing very little to make sure bee farmers get access to the equipment they need.

Also, there is a huge gap in the research involving the existing beekeeping technologies, equipment, honeybee, and product utilization. Without this proper and intense research, it is nearly impossible for beekeeping to grow or become lucrative for new people willing to join in.

#: Getting your first bee colony

Another key area that most new or future beekeepers find a challenge is finding the first bee colony.

Finding your first bee colony is usually through one of these three ways: either by buying nucs locally, trapping wild swarms, or buying packaged and shipped bees. Therefore, it usually poses a challenge, especially for beginners, to find the best way to get their first bees.

It is advisable that as a new beekeeper, buying a nuc box locally from local beekeepers is the best way to go. Doing this reduces the stress and trouble of trapping your bees or shipping them. However, you can choose the best way that suits you.

#: *Nectar dearth*

One of the most problematic issues you can face is nectar dearth because it may lead to a honey shortage. Nectar dearth is when there is a shortage of nectar-producing flowers. That usually happens during winter, and for a beginner, this can be a big challenge.

Aside from causing a shortage of nectar-producing flowers, a strong colony might try to rob a weaker colony of their nectar stores. Another consequence is the transfer of parasites like Varroa mite from the weak colony to the strong colony.

If you notice nectar dearth, try feeding your bees syrup, reducing entrance to the colony, and putting up community feeders near your apiary.

#: *Beehive placement confusion*

Deciding where to keep your beehive can be quite the challenge, especially for beginners, especially now that chemical products, climate change, and the economy have a tangible impact on our activities as beekeepers.

Most new beekeepers tend to start in their yard, but this is easy only when you live outside the city. If you live surrounded by neighbors or near the road, then you will encounter challenges.

Here is the bottom line:

Never place an apiary at a location where it can cause a potential risk to other people, animals, or the bees themselves.

That is a small sampling of the most common challenges you are likely to face as a budding beekeeper and some of the solutions you can explore.

Before you can start your journey towards becoming a beekeeper, you'd do well to consider how legal it is to keep bees in your locality/residential area.

Is Beekeeping Legal In My City?

Whether you're interested in beekeeping because of adding pollinators to your farm or garden, harvesting honey/beeswax, or just out of curiosity, there are things you need to keep in mind.

First, before you get started, you would do well to ask yourself one important question: *is beekeeping legal in my city?*

It would be a shame to buy all the supplies and use up all your resources only for you to have a run-in with the law. Fortunately, most cities allow beekeeping, but some ordinances put restrictions on beekeeping, such as how many hives you should have.

To help you with the legality of beekeeping in your area, here are some tips you can try.

Search your City's Government website

One place you can find resourceful information is your government's websites. By searching for it over the Internet, you'll find lots of information regarding ordinances and laws. For example, if you're wondering how legal beekeeping is in your city, then your City's website is a good place to look.

Contact your State Agricultural department

In any state, the state department of agriculture is most likely to be handling beekeeping ordinances. And so, contacting them by phone or physically would be a good place to start to learn about the legalities of beekeeping in your city.

If all else fails, you can consider giving your city clerk a call. They should be in a better position to direct you to the proper resources.

Beekeeping Laws By State

If you happen to be living in the US, here are some links to the information you need about beekeeping in your city.

Alabama

https://bit.ly/3wfSpkT

Alaska

https://bit.ly/3pVRqnL

Arizona

https://bit.ly/3pJtP9y

Arkansas

https://bit.ly/3zkMLQo

California

https://bit.ly/2TQEmnq

Colorado

https://bit.ly/3zkDHes

Connecticut

https://bit.ly/3vg0rJl

Delaware

https://bit.ly/3vhgm9Y

Florida

https://bit.ly/3gfgx1j

Georgia

https://bit.ly/3ggZOLj

Hawaii

https://bit.ly/3xfMhsV

Idaho

https://bit.ly/3vcDW7T

Illinois

https://bit.ly/3wb9s7D

Iowa

https://bit.ly/3wb9s7D

Kansas

https://bit.ly/3gw2lQJ

Kentucky

https://bit.ly/3cD3iFI

Louisiana

https://bit.ly/2RMuTNt

Maine

https://bit.ly/3vfpxry

Maryland

https://bit.ly/3gg0tzs

Massachusetts

https://bit.ly/3pR3tT5

Michigan

https://bit.ly/2RLCADr

Minnesota

https://bit.ly/2RKl6r4

Mississippi

https://bit.ly/3pNjDgq

Missouri

https://bit.ly/35bGQ29

Montana

https://bit.ly/3zir4QR

Nebraska

https://bit.ly/3gur5bJ

Nevada

https://bit.ly/3pHNN4u

New Hampshire

https://bit.ly/2TnW0og

New Jersey

https://bit.ly/3vgcUwn

New Mexico

https://bit.ly/3ggxjNS

New York

https://on.ny.gov/2RKkdib

North Carolina

https://bit.ly/3xgNJLK

North Dakota

https://bit.ly/2Tnz4zL

Ohio

https://bit.ly/3zjzuaO

Oklahoma

https://bit.ly/3zmMNak

Oregon

https://bit.ly/2SrxwVa

Pennsylvania

https://bit.ly/3wifzaa

Rhode Island

https://bit.ly/3zjHatr

South Carolina

https://bit.ly/3cCcHNz

South Dakota

https://bit.ly/2RLDC2h

Tennessee

https://bit.ly/3pJRuqe

Texas

https://bit.ly/3czjpnJ

Utah

https://bit.ly/3vhZrEp

Vermont

https://bit.ly/2TUlILn

Virginia

https://bit.ly/359sEXF

Washington

https://bit.ly/2Tn5ytE

West Virginia

https://bit.ly/2RJkpyc

Wisconsin

https://bit.ly/3gd3PAk

Wyoming

https://bit.ly/3pGOVFC

Contact your local beekeepers' association

If you live in an area that is serious about beekeeping, they are most likely to have a beekeepers association. So, you can inquire with them about the laws or ordinances surrounding beekeeping in your area.

It is important to note that each city has its own laws and ordinances. Thus, ensure that the laws or ordinances you use apply to your city or area by checking with the options listed above.

The Cost of Beekeeping

Although beekeeping is a lucrative activity to engage yourself in, there is also the point of what it will cost you to become a fully-fledged beekeeper. Considering this is especially important because it helps you in planning and managing your beehives.

If you do a rough survey over the Internet, you'll see that you need a minimum of roughly $725 per hive in the first year. A set of hive components usually costs about $275. Basic tools and protective gear usually cost $165. A bee package is usually roughly $150. Miscellaneous costs for sales and supplies are approximately $150.

However, this is just an approximate of the total cost. The real cost will depend on where you get your supplies.

The variables that will affect your total cost of beekeeping include:

- The size of your initial colony.
- The kind of beehive configuration you plan to use.
- The beekeepers involved.
- Where you are going to place your hives.

- The protection you're going to use for your beehives.
- The type of bee package you are going to get.

How Many Beekeepers Involved?

Depending on how many beekeepers will participate in the beekeeping endeavor, you will need:

Protective clothing

The number of beekeepers you have will automatically dictate the cost of protective clothing you'll get.

As a beginner, you cannot risk not wearing protective gear because you might end up hurting yourself. Protective gear usually consists of a veil to protect your eyes and face, a full bee suit, or a bee jacket and gloves.

The product design and the level of protection you choose will affect your cost. Costs usually vary, but mostly, the minimum outlay of protective gear ranges from $90 - $120.

You can buy these from Amazon or your local store.

Beekeeping Tools

There are some very important tools that every beginner should have; these are a bee smoker, a hive tool, and a bee brush.

You can find all these (a bee smoker, a hive tool, and a bee brush) from Amazon and many other retailers.

Beehive Configuration

For beginners, the Langstroth hive is the best. These are the most commonly used hives in North America. These hives usually consist of boxes that are vertically stacked with the same width and length. Each of the boxes usually consists of a foundation and frames where the bees build their wax comb.

The cost of a fairly popular hive arrangement for ten frame boxes includes:

- Bottom board as the base
- Two honey supers
- 10 frames per box with foundation
- Two deep broad boxes

You can buy these from Amazon or your local store.

You can buy the boxes and frames as assembled and unassembled. However, it is much cheaper to buy unassembled components, but it is advisable to buy an assembled one for a beginner.

So, based on the average costs, you need roughly $260-270 per hive.

How Many Colonies and in Which Format?

When you start as a beekeeper, you might consider getting only one colony to minimize the risk. If you do everything right and all goes well, then you might never need another bee colony. However, things happen, and to be on the safe side, you'll need another colony.

That's why if your budget allows it, then you need to start with two colonies to increase your odds of not having to restart in your second year.

Getting bees usually happens in two main formats:

1. **A bee nuc, or nucleus colony:** A nuc is a small hive that usually consists of 5 frames with nectar, Queens, bees, comb, and e.t.c. They are usually more expensive because they come together with the frames and require more effort and time to create. If you happen to find a local nuc that has overwintered and is available, then get those to help improve your gene pool and increase the odds of your colony surviving the next winter.

2. **Package bees:** These usually consist of a small box of bees weighing around 3 pounds, including a caged queen. The bees are normally transferred en masse to your hive after receiving them.

Generally, packaged bees are relatively cheaper than overwintered nucs.

Cost of bees

Format	High	Low	Average
Bee package	$200.00	$125.00	$150.00
Spring nuc	$220.00	$180.00	$194.00
Overwintered	$250.00	$210.00	$228.00

A nuc is the best option for a beginner because it is easy to install; a nuc also has the highest survival rate.

Hive Stand

When you decide to get a beehive, you cannot just place it on the ground; instead, you will need to use a stand to help protect it from running water and harsh climates such as winter.

You can make your hive with as little as a few cinder blocks and lumber, as these are more than enough for the job. If you're looking to cut costs, you can always make a hive stand or if you're not capable, purchase the one that suits your needs.

Just make sure to lift your hives at least 18 inches off the ground and get a stand that can support up to 200 pounds.

You can buy hive stands from Amazon and other retailers online or offline:

Varroa Mite Treatment

As you start keeping bees, you will most probably have to deal with a Varroa destructor mites. This major pest can destroy your entire colony.

There are various treatment options at your disposal to deal with this; options include quick strips, oxalic acid, and mite away, two of which you'll have to buy, while some treatments you'll require additional equipment. Therefore, be prepared to handle this cost in your first year and after that.

The estimated annual cost for treating varroa mite in your first year is around $25 per hive.

However, the cost might be higher if you decide to use vaporized oxalic acid in your first year. A good vaporizer can cost about $150 to almost $500. Moreover, to ensure your safety while using a vaporizer, you must wear a face mask to avoid vapor inhalation.

Time cost

When you think about cost, you might only be thinking about dollars and cents. However, the time you spend on beekeeping is also an incurred cost.

The time function combines many things, such as how long it takes to do a hive inspection, how much assembly work you do, the challenges you face, etc.

Therefore, if you decide to be a beekeeper, allot enough time to maintain your apiary healthy and growing. Then, once you're done taking your bees through winter, you'll have a lot of time to relax.

Animal protection

Your beehive will face challenges due to the snow and small animals like skunks, raccoons, and mice. These animals can disrupt your bees, making them irritable. They can also knock over your hives, causing a lot of damage. Sometimes, especially during winter, it is possible for mice to climb up into your hive, build a nest there and then grow a family.

Therefore, you need some extra layer of protection, especially if you're in an area prone to these animals. You can use lashing straps or ratchet straps to hold your hive in place should it attempt to topple over, and it is relatively inexpensive. They are also quite handy when tying down your covers if you live in a cold place or an area prone to storm winds. Free stones can also do the trick.

Bears are also very destructive animals when it comes to beekeeping. Besides loving honey and bees, bears also love the bee brood. Therefore, the best way to protect your hive/s from bears is to set up an electric fence, something fundamental if you live in an area prone to them. An electric fence is better than a regular fence because bears can climb over the letter or burrow under it.

A small electric fence can cost anywhere from $200-300. However, that is only necessary if you're in an area prone to animals especially bears.

Winterization

Any seasoned beekeeper will tell you that getting your bees through winter is an important aspect of beekeeping. You must take measures to help your bees survive through winter. Some beekeepers choose to wrap their hives in tar paper to cut down the wind penetrating.

But just to be on the safe side, you can place a screen board with sugar bricks under the inner cover and some burlap to absorb condensation. Add some additional insulation above the inner covers before wrapping the hives in a bee cozy.

The cost of winterization might be relatively cheaper in a warm climate but make sure to protect your bees from harsh climates to avoid colony losses. During cold climates, winterization cost varies from $50 to $75 depending on what you do.

Miscellaneous Costs

Just like in any activity you might undertake, it is important to keep in mind that there will always be extra costs that you might not have anticipated. Therefore, it is important to budget for miscellaneous costs depending on your circumstances and region.

The rough estimate for miscellaneous costs is about $75, a rough estimate of various, somewhat universal items like sugar and pollen patties, paint, and other equipment.

How to Save on Beekeeping

If you'd like to kick start your beekeeping at a lower cost, you might consider starter kits because they are cheaper than buying everything ala carte. Unfortunately, some might be on the lower end when it comes to the quality spectrum, but they are fine for beginners.

However, make sure to be careful because some kits are misleading. Just make sure that the kits have all the required equipment and at a favorable price.

Also, be on the lookout for supplier specials and offers. This might allow you to get all you need at a relatively discounted price.

If you have some basic tools and woodworking skills, you may enjoy some DIY projects that significantly reduce the price. You can have fun making some hives and other structures that you may need.Buying locally assembled hives or equipment can save you the shipping fee.

However, it is best not to buy used hives unless they come from a reputable source. Even then, the seller should be willing to renovate the hive to avoid cross colony contamination.

Many factors determine the cost of beekeeping because the cost will depend on many factors personalized to your needs. However, knowing what you need and how much they cost will allow you to budget for costs and make informed decisions.

Other Beekeeping Considerations

Let's now look at other important considerations before getting into beekeeping.

If you or your neighbor has allergies

Although this sounds like an obvious thing, those allergic to bee stings or pollen should stay away from bees. Even with the protective gear and equipment, you are prone to stings.

The same case applies to those living with you and also around your home (neighbors). For example, you might find that the person living next door to you is allergic to bee stings, which puts them at risk should you happen to keep the bees. Therefore, it is important to investigate if your neighbors have any allergies related to bees or mind having the bees around.

Even if you don't have allergies yourself, you need to ask yourself if you mind getting stung. If you do get stung, the quickest remedy is to slather the sting with baking soda paste.

Are you willing to put in the work?

The other most important consideration is to ask yourself if you can handle beekeeping. Only you can know if you have the energy, time, and resources required to become a seasoned beekeeper.

Taking time to consider this is particularly important because if you're not an active person or are the type of person who indulges in things fast and gives them up just as fast, you might want to reconsider. However, if you are excited and ready to do what it takes despite the many challenges of beekeeping, then you're good to go.

Also, if you live the snowbird lifestyle where you travel frequently, or you're only in an area occasionally, you won't manage to take good care of your hives.

Failure is normal in beekeeping. Therefore, unless you're prepared to fail and continue regardless of failures, then the fortitude to stick might not be there.

These and all the other factors mentioned above are what you should have in mind before getting started in beekeeping. At first, it might sound like a lot, but once you get used to it, it will be a walk in the park.

Let's now look at the science surrounding bees and their entire ecosystem.

Chapter 2

Bee Hierarchy & The Hive

As you already know or will learn shortly, bees are social animals. Therefore, they live in family groups that are large and organized well. Normally, social insects are pretty advanced and are capable of doing things that solitary insects don't do.

The most apparent way to see this is in most of the survival behaviors that honey bees have developed, such as nest construction, communication, defense, division of labor, and environmental control. These behaviors are what make social insects such as bees wonderful creatures.

Therefore, as a beekeeper, there is a need to learn more about the hierarchy of bees and how they operate so that you can be best suited to handle them. First, a honey bee colony usually involves three types of adult bees namely drones, workers, and a queen.

Each of these members has a specially designed role in the colony in relation to its adult age. However, surviving and reproducing requires the combined efforts of the entire colony. Which only means that individual bees cannot survive without the entire colony.

Worker bees usually come together to collect food, rear brood and build nests. On the other hand, the presence of a queen and drones maintains the colony.

The colony usually depends on communicative dances and chemical pheromones among workers to communicate and increase the chances of survival. A colony's strength and reproductiveness depend on the quantity of food reserves, the queen, and the workforce size. The efficiency of the colony grows as the size increases to a maximum of about 60,000 workers.

That was just a general outlook of how bees work; here is a more detailed explanation of the characteristics of each individual in a bee colony.

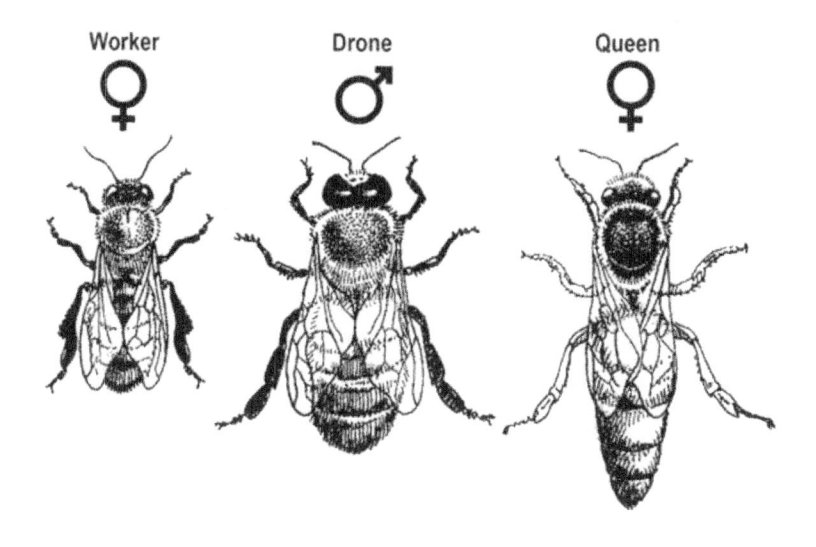

The Queen

The queen is the most important individual in any colony. Thus, each colony usually has only one queen except during supersedure and swarming preparation. This is because she is the only developed female and her primary function is reproduction; without her, the colony cannot grow.

The queen can produce both fertilized and unfertilized eggs, and these queens usually lay most eggs during early summer or spring. You can easily know if the queen is at her peak production when she lays about 1500 eggs a day. That means a queen can produce up to 250000 eggs each year and possibly more than a million in her entire lifetime.

You can easily distinguish a queen from other bees due to her body which is much longer than either the worker's or the drone's, especially during the egg-laying period when her abdomen appears greatly elongated.

A queen's thorax is usually slightly larger than that of a worker, and she has neither functional wax glands nor pollen baskets. In addition, her wings only cover about two-thirds of her abdomen, while those of drones and workers nearly reach the tip of the abdomen when covered.

The stinger on a queen bee is normally curved and longer than that of the workers, but it has fewer and shorter barbs.

The average productive lifespan is 2 to 3 years, but sometimes they can live up to 5 years.

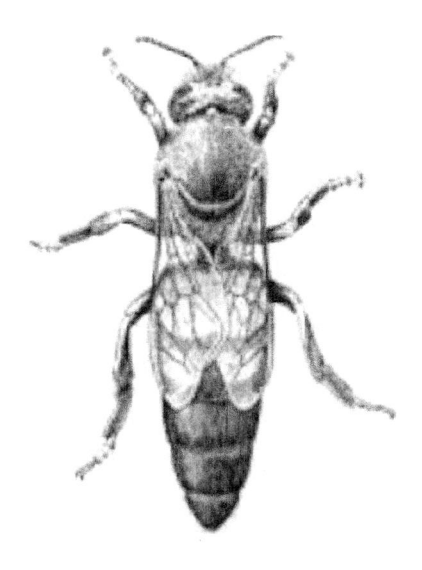

A queen bees' other important function is producing pheromones that glue the colony together and give each bee a sense of belonging. One of the major pheromones she produces, mostly known as queen substance, is produced by her mandibular glands even though others are important. Her genetic makeup and that of the drone she has mated are key to determining the colony's size, quality, and temperament.

A week after the queen emerges from her queen cell, she has to leave the hive and go mate with several drones in flight. So to avoid inbreeding, she needs to fly some distance from her colony, approximately 13 minutes away alone.

She first circles the hive she's interested in in the afternoon, with 7 to 15 drones, the queen mates at an altitude above 20 feet. The drones can locate the queen because of the chemical odor she emits, enabling them to find as well as recognize her.

When bad weather causes a delay in the queen mating flight for over 20 days, she then loses her mating ability and can only be able to lay eggs that are not fertilized, which results in drones only.

Once the queen has mated, she returns to her hive and begins laying the eggs within 48 hours. She then releases sperms from her spermatheca every time she lays an egg that can later become a queen or a worker. If she lays an egg in a cell the size of a drone, she won't release sperms.

The workers constantly attend and feed royal jelly to their queen because the number of eggs she lays directly relates to how much food she gets and the workforce size that can prepare the beeswax cells for her eggs within three days. If the queen substance secreted by the queen is inadequate, the workers prepare to replace her (supersede) by putting the queen and her new daughter together in the hive for a while after supersedure.

New queens (virgins) usually develop from fertilized eggs or not more than three-day-old young worker larvae. Queens develop from three main circumstances emergency, supersedure, or swarming.

If, for some reason, the old queen gets removed, lost, or accidentally killed, the colony replaces her by creating emergency queens from younger worker larvae. These queens then grow up—or get raised—in vertical structures modified by the bees to hang on the comb surface.

However, queens developed from supersedure are much better than emergency queens because they receive larger quantities of food from development. Like emergency queen cells raised on the comb surface, supersedure queens also receive the same treatment.

On the other hand, queen cells produced during swarming preparation are found in the gaps of the beeswax combs or along the margins of the frames within the brood area.

Workers

The workers are the smallest individuals in any colony and occupy the most space. They are sexually underdeveloped females and, therefore, under normal hive conditions, don't lay eggs.

These workers have specialized structures such as scent glands, pollen baskets, food glands, and wax glands. That's why they can perform all the labors of the hive.

Most of their duties include removing debris, cleaning and polishing the cells, guarding the entrance, caring for the queen, feeding the brood, ventilating the hive, and handling incoming nectar. Later, when they become field bees, they forage for nectar, pollen, propolis, and water.

The lifespan of an average worker bee during summer is about six weeks. However, workers reared during the fall can live up to 6 months by rearing new generations in the spring and allowing the colony to survive the winter.

WORKER BEE

Laying Workers

If a colony becomes queen-less for any reason, the ovaries of most of the workers develop, and they begin to lay unfertilized eggs. The workers' ovaries don't develop until something happens to the queen because many beekeepers believe that the presence of the brood, queen, and her chemicals impede that.

Therefore, having egg-laying workers in a colony means that the queen has been absent for more than two weeks. However, the workers laying eggs does not just happen when the queen is gone. It also happens during the swarming season when a poor queen heads the colony.

You can easily recognize colonies with workers laying eggs because you might notice 5 to 15 eggs per cell while small bodies of drones are in worker-sized cells.

Furthermore, worker bees usually lay their eggs all over the brood combs, and therefore, you can find the eggs on the sides of the cell instead of at the base, where a queen would place them. However, most of these eggs don't hatch, and for drone larvae that survive, it does not survive to maturity inside the smaller cells.

Drone Bees

While the worker bees are the female versions of bees, drones are male bees whose sole purpose is to mate with the queen. They don't even sting; they don't work and don't make honey. And since most queens only need to mate once, most of the drones don't even get to fulfill their role. However, worker bees keep them around anyway in case a new queen needs mating.

These drones usually live for about eight weeks, and during that time, they get their needs met by worker bees. However, when fall comes, the worker bees kick them out of the colony to save their resources and energy.

You can recognize drones because they look stouter and a little longer than worker bees. Also, their eyes are twice as big as the worker bees' eyes because drones need good sight when they have to follow the queen up in the air.

When a queen flies into the appropriate height, hundreds and sometimes thousands of drones compete to mate with the queen. They don't do that through fighting, but who can fly closest to mate successfully.

It's very tempting to think that these drones are pretty much useless. However, aside from reproduction, drones play a great role in the future of the colony's/bees' genetic diversity. Also, when the hive temperatures rise, the drones can help with the cooling effect by flapping their wings.

They can also serve a purpose to you as a beekeeper because when you see them in early spring, you'll know swarm season has begun.

Bee Development Stages

All honey bees go through three essential development stages before emerging as adults. They start with egg then larva and then pupa before becoming adults. These 3 stages collectively make up what is referred to brood, and while the development stages are similar, the durations differ. Fertilized eggs become queens or workers, while unfertilized eggs become drones.

Nutrition also plays a great role in the development stages because queen larva receives copious amounts of royal jelly. In contrast, workers tend to get less amount of royal jelly and more of a mixture of pollen and honey.

The Bee Cycle

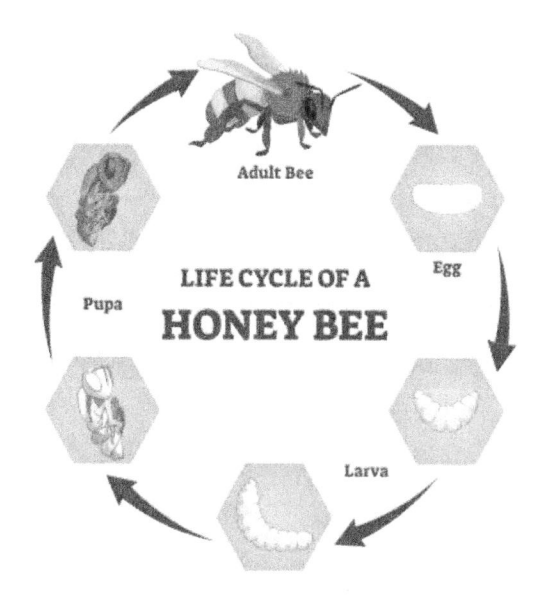

Eggs

The queen usually lays one egg per cell, with each egg attached to the bottom of the cell. It usually looks like a tiny grain of rice. The main criteria for determining whether an egg becomes male or female is whether it gets fertilized.

When the queen lays the egg, it stands up straight on end. However, during the three-day development period, it begins to bend over. Finally, on the third day, the eggs hatch, beginning the larval stage.

Larvae

You can figure out if a larva is healthy if the appearance is white and it has a glistening glow. Larvae usually assume the shape of a "C" on the bottom of the cells. The queen, worker, and drone cells get covered after the 5 ½, 6, and 61/2 days, respectively. During this entire period, they are usually fed by worker bees while inside the cells. We call the period before the cell gets capped a prepupal stage.

While in this period, the larva is grub-like in appearance but stretches itself apart and can spin a thin silken cocoon. Also, the larvae remain plump, pearly white, and glistening during the entire period.

Pupae

Inside the individual cells covered in a beeswax cover provided by the adult worker, their pre-pupae evolve from their Laval form to adult bees. A healthy pupa remains glistening and white during the first stages of development even though their bodies have already started taking on adult form.

The first organs to get their color are the compound eyes that change from white to brownish-purple. Soon after, the color of the entire body starts to look more like that of an adult bee. Queens, drones, and workers emerge 7 1/2, 14 ½, and 12 days respectively after cell capping.

Seasonal Cycles of Activities in Colonies

Now that you've known honey bee groupings, it is only fair to learn what exactly happens inside the beehives and among the colonies.

A normal colony usually has a queen, a cluster of 60,000 workers, and several hundred drones. The cluster usually stays over several wax combs used to store pollen and honey and rear young bees to replace old adults.

The activities of any colony depend on the seasons; for example, the period between September to December is usually like a new year for the colony because the condition of the colony affects the prosperity for the next year.

In the fall, the amounts of pollen and nectar entering the hive fall, leading to a reduction in the population and brood rearing. The proportion of the old bees in the colony usually decreases depending on the queen's age and egg-laying condition. However, the young bees survive the winter while the old ones slowly die. The worker bees insulate the hive using the collected propolis to seal all cracks in the hive and reduce the entrance to keep out the cold air.

When the nectar becomes scarce for whatever reason, the workers chase the drones out of the hive, which causes them to starve and die. When the temperatures drop to about 57° F, the worker bees decide to form a tighter cluster. The brood is kept warm at about 93° F, which is the heat generated by the bees. This egg-laying process tapers off completely as you approach October and November, even if the pollen gets stored in the combs. However, egg-laying and brood-rearing usually never stops during tropical, subtropical, and mild winter conditions.

When the temperatures fall, the bees draw closer to conserve heat by compressing the outer layer within the cluster. Therefore, the cluster expands and contracts as the temperature rises and falls. Thus, the bees living inside the hive have access to the food stores during the entire period. When the warm periods arrive, the cluster shifts its position to cover new areas of the comb. This means that an extremely prolonged cold spell will prohibit the movement of the cluster, and the bees can starve to death.

The queen always remains within the cluster and only moves when it shifts positions. The bees lost during winter get replaced when the queen starts laying eggs during late December or early January. The pollen gathered during the previous fall determines early brooding, which delays if the colonies lack pollen. The population of bees usually decreases significantly during winter because old bees die, and young bees bred with ample pollen and honey have a strong population.

Swarming

Before the first virgin queen is almost ready and before the main nectar flow, the colony usually swarms during the warmer part of the day. This usually happens when the queen and half the bees rush en masse out of the hive entrance. They fly around for several minutes before clustering on a limb of a tree or something similar. The cluster remains in that position for about an hour, depending on how soon scouting bees can find a new location. Then, once the scouts locate a new location, the cluster breaks and flies to that location.

The worker bees start working on the hive as soon as they get there by brood rearing, gathering pollen and pollen, and constructing combs. This process, called swarming, usually occurs from March to June.

When the swarm departs from its parent colony, the remaining bees continue their fieldwork, including collecting water, propolis, nectar, and pollen. They conduct all their roles to keep the hive running. Male bees receive nurturing care because they'll need to mate with the virgin queen. After she emerges from her cell, the first thing she does is to eat honey and groom herself before she proceeds to look for other rival queens inside the colony.

The queens fight each other until only one queen remains, and a week after, she flies out to mate with drones in the air. As soon as the drones mate with the queen, they die. The queen then returns to the nest soon after as the New Queen Mother. Then the cycle continues.

In the hot summer days, the colony's temperature must be about 93°F, if the colony is to survive. The worker bees do this by gathering water and spreading it across the entire area inside the nest.

During early summer, the colony is at its peak population. And so, instead, the bees focus on collecting pollen and nectar and storing honey as part of winter preparedness. During summer, bees attempt to store enough honey, which is when, as a beekeeper, you can remove a portion and still leave ample honey for colony survival.

Spring Activity

When spring comes, brood rearing increases because of the lengthening days and new pollen and nectar sources. In addition, the bees collect water to regulate the temperature and liquefy thickened honey during the preparation of brood food. However, during this period, drones are made scarce or absent during this time of the year.

During later in the spring, the colony's population expands drastically while the population of young bees increases significantly. And as the population increases, so does the field worker force, which means greater amounts of nectar and pollen than needed to maintain the rear brooding.

With the days increasing and the temperature as well, the cluster grows together more and more with the drones, which causes the colony to be overcrowded. That is usually evident if you happen to spot more bees at the entrance hanging in a cluster on a warm day.

Together with these crowded conditions, the queen prepares for division during swarming by laying drone eggs. In addition to rearing the drones and workers, the bees also prepare a new queen that will remain behind. This usually happens when a few larvae that would otherwise grow to become worker bees eat jelly in order to reconstruct and become the new queen. Eating jelly ends up speeding up her development.

Even if the colony becomes overcrowded, the bees will not divide and swarm until they are ready. So the colony tries at first to expand by building combs as long as room and food are available. The new combs constructed usually work as storage facilities for brood rearing and pollen storage.

That is just about everything you need to know about each member in a bee colony and their activities throughout the year. Knowing this is particularly important in monitoring your colony and understanding what exactly is going on.

Now that you've known how bees work, let's get you started on building the perfect beehive for you.

Chapter 3

A Home For Your Bees

Before you jump into building a beehive/s, it is important to figure out which kind of beekeeper you are. This is crucial because it will determine the specifications of the beehive.

Here is a detailed explanation of the different kinds of beekeepers, how you can know if you fit the description, and the corresponding beehive configuration ideal for each.

Most people don't even know that there are different types of beekeepers and that within these types, there are several beekeeping styles. Here are the three common types of beekeepers. Which one describes you?

The Modern Commercial Beekeeper

This beekeeper usually uses roach baits in high traps, chemical mite traps, feeds bees fructose corn syrup, and even makes hives die especially during the process of almond pollination.

The idea of a modern beekeeper is not to harm the bees but to help ensure their health for great returns. Here are the pros and cons of a modern commercial beekeeper to help you decide.

Pros

- Massive amounts of honey and pollen production, which means more income
- More experience in the short term

Cons

- Having to rebuild constantly due to colony losses
- The equipment is expensive
- The quality of the honey is low due to the chemicals
- Usually, a very non bee friendly approach
- Has many expenses
- Constantly dealing with hive pests and diseases.

The Treatment-free Beekeeper

Just like the title suggests, this kind of beekeeping usually dictates that you don't use any treatment. Instead, you can help better your bees and yourself depending on the beehive configuration you use.

If you decide to be this kind of beekeeper, you have to avoid using Langstroth style beehives, especially interior plastic designs. This is because the comb, which is the foundation of the health of your beehive, is not cycled enough to maintain a homeostatic environment.

This means that this kind of beekeeper would do better using the Warre or Top Bar Style beehives. This is where there is constant harvesting of the comb.

Remember that the health of your colony is important. Therefore, the first step is allowing the bees to make new combs when necessary. When you use chemicals and pesticides, they get stored in older combs that create a foundation for poor health. Here are the pros and cons of being this kind of beekeeper.

Pros

- Reduced labor for the beekeeper.
- Less in-hive disturbance and interference.
- It reduces the personal time to care for the hive and fewer expenses on the supplies needed.

Cons

- Reduced amounts of honey.
- Generally, the bees are less productive.

- The hives are difficult to keep alive.

- Reduced success in maintaining the health of an apiary.

- Constantly have to deal with pests and diseases.

The Chemical-free Beekeeper Who Treats

Unlike the previous form of beekeeping, this method requires the beekeeper to use non-harmful intervention, mainly because he/she is aware of the many challenges a modern bee faces, which is why they try to help them out.

Therefore, this means that instead of using harmful treatments, for example, in treating varroa mites, you choose a thermosolar or oxalic acid treatment. A beekeeper following this method requires extensive research to make sure they are aware of their many alternatives.

This type of beekeeping works best with a Top Bar and Langstroth style beehives. They are both best suited for this type because they allow for an easier hive inspection.

Pros

- It gives the bees a stronger ability to make a crop and forage

- It gives the bees a chance for the need to thrive as a colony.

- Allows for the beekeeper to be in constant supervision of the hive.

- It increases the chances of having a harvestable crop.

Cons

- If not done correctly, the bees can get harmed.

- The tools required can get pricey.

- Some methods are unusable with honey in the hive.

These are the three kinds of beekeepers you can be. So it is up to you to figure out what best works for you. The next thing for you to learn is the best beehive configurations at your disposal.

First:

What Is A Beehive?

A beehive is where bees live and make their products, usually in an artificial box or an empty hollow log. However, when the bees are in the wild, they usually create a nest in a hollow tree.

A tree may be home to bees for years and years, but only if Varroa mites don't wipe them out. Also, not every bee that lives in a tree is a beehive. It's very easy to confuse hornet nests with honey beehives.

The only other kind of beehive that exists is the one made by humans. We often use the term apiary to describe a group of hives in one location. Putting the hives together makes for a better bee management strategy. However, it is advisable not to put many colonies in one place.

A beehive usually has two structures: the outside physical structure that encloses the nest and the inside physical structure. The honeycombs made from beeswax make up the second component of the hive. These honeycombs are sheets containing thousands of individual wax cells often shaped like a hexagon.

Inside the beehive

What happens inside a beehive is that bees make beeswax from the underside of their abdomen. It usually takes a lot of work and energy, but they get it done as quickly as possible.

Inside the wax cells, honey bees usually make and store honey which they use over winter. The pollen collected by the bees also gets converted to bee bread and stored until the colony needs it. The wax cells are also useful in holding developing bee babies, known as brood.

The interior of a beehive is often sticky because of the presence of propolis. Propolis is a combined mixture of saliva, resins, and beeswax, which has anti-fungal and anti-inflammatory properties. Excessive propolis makes it hard for any beekeeper to assess a beehive because of the stickiness but the more the propolis, the healthier the bees.

The Most Common Beehive Configurations

Here are the most common types of beehives you can get.

1: Langstroth hive

This is the most common and widely used beehive among all the beehives. The design was created by Rev. Lorenzo Langstroth around mid-century and features removable frames where the bees can build their comb. This hive configuration consists of boxes stacked together on top of each other.

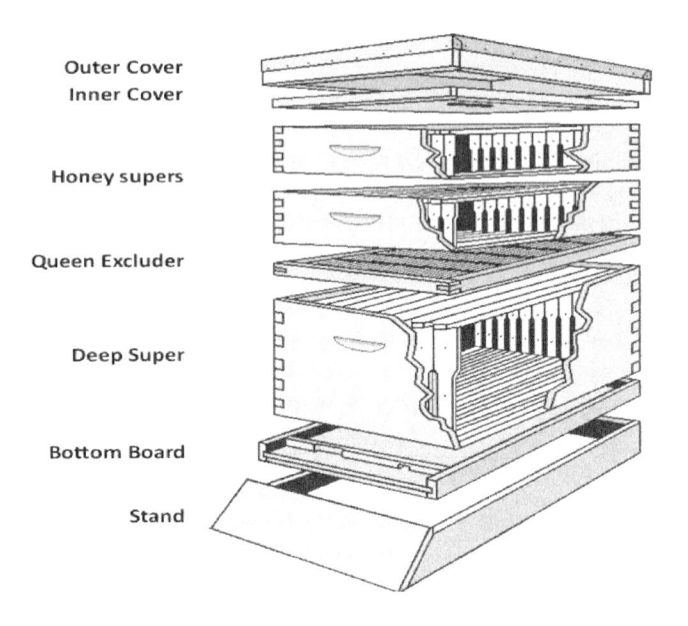

Parts of a Langstroth hive

- **Telescoping/outer cover** - this part is important for keeping the hive dry and covering the entire structure.

- **Honey/shallow supers-** this is where the production of honey usually occurs.

- **Inner cover-** This the part between the outer and top hive box that provides insulation and prevents the frames from the outer cover. It sometimes acts as an escape route for bees during honey harvesting.

- **Frames** - these are wooden or plastic structures that fit the three different sizes of supers. Also, this is where the bees build honeycombs, which, in turn, hold young ones, nectar, and pollen.

- **Brood chamber-** this is usually where the queen lays her eggs; it consists of larger frames than the shallow super.

- **Foundation-** the foundation is often used to encourage bees to construct straight combs inside the frames. Beekeepers use sheets of beeswax as a guide inside the frames.

- **Bottom board** - this part is usually the base of the hive.

This hive configuration can combine the three sizes of super boxes: deep, shallow, or medium.

Pros

- It's easy to extract honey from the hive.
- It can easily be dissected, inspected, and manipulated.

- The parts and hives are usually readily available.
- It's the most used in beekeeping training.

Cons

- It is usually time-consuming when waxing and wiring the frames.
- It has a lot of work in measuring and cutting precisely to stop the bees from filling the gaps.
- The wax combs absorb pesticides and metal over time.
- It provides lots of places for pests to hide.
- It has many fidgeting bits and parts

Many beepeers consider this a commercial beehive, making it not ideal for backyard beekeeping.

2: *Warrè hive*

This beehive configuration built by Èmile warrè in the mid-20th century is yet another top bar design. However, instead of being a long top horizontal bar, this hive is a vertical top bar hive. It usually has identical-sized stacked boxes that have no foundation or frames.

The bees usually build their honeycombs down from top bars strategically placed inside each box.

The beekeepers that use this design normally place their supers at the bottom instead of putting empty boxes at the top to give the bees more headroom. That makes the design more like the beehives in the wild.

Pros

- The design facilitates free airflow because of the natural vortex created by the shape.

- The design is easy to construct.

- It encourages the bees to build their natural honeycomb.
- It gives the queen full access to the entire space.

Cons

- The frames for this design are not available to buy and are challenging to construct.
- Every time you want to add a new box under two or more full boxes, you'll need a lifting device.
- If you use frames, pests can easily get a hidden place.
- Access to this hive is only through taking the roof off.

This hive design is a great hive for bees and beekeepers.

3: Top bar hive

This is considered the oldest design, with wooden bars laid on top of the long box. However, unlike the four-sided wooden bars used in the Langstroth design, one-piece bars are used instead.

The benefits of a top bar hive are that no wooden frames are required to assemble, and no sheet foundations are required. In addition, managing a top bar hive is much easier than the

Langstroth hive because it does not require moving several heavy boxes.

Although this hive is great for producing honey, most beekeepers use it for pollination alone.

Top bar hives need regular inspections to avoid overcrowding or swarming. Also, it's not possible to use a centrifugal honey extractor, which means the honey and the comb manual removal.

Pros

- The hive allows for easy inspection because of the shape of the hive.

- Allows the bees to build their comb according to the colony's needs.

- The design does not require heavy lifting, and extraction of honey is easy.

- It allows for the addition of supers.

Cons

- They are not readily available and not easy to construct.

- Very few people use this beehive configuration which makes its development difficult.

4: The long/horizontal hive

If you'd rather have a horizontal design that will help put your heavy lifting days behind you, then the long hive is a great fit. The design mimics that of a Langstroth hive, but the difference is the arrangement. A Langstroth is stacked vertically while the long hive is stacked horizontally.

Therefore, this beehive configuration is perfect for short or disabled people. Since the boxes are not stacked, no heavy lifting is required.

In some cases, this design usually entails an observation window that makes it easier to check on your bees, especially during winter, without having to open up the entire hive.

Pros

- You can use the frames of Langstroth interchangeably.

- No heavy lifting is required since everything is on the same level.

- The modified version of this hive allows the addition of supers.

- It offers space to place your tools as you inspect your hive.

Cons

- Aside from the frames, no other fixtures can fit with this hive.

- They are relatively more expensive than other hives because they are not easy to find.

5: Dome hive

This design draws inspiration from the centricity of the bee of the sun hive. Because this is a curve-topped hive, you can hang it anywhere from a tree or pole and even set it up on a tripod stand.

In the hive, there are top ten bars for honeycombs and 2 for ventilation. It usually consists of 101 pieces of kiln pine dried and assembled into a top dome, a bottom dome, and a central ring.

Pros

- It gives the queen full access to the hive.

- The round shape of the hive facilitates a healthy and strong colony.

- There is no room for pests to hide because of the smooth surface.

- The design allows the top dome to lift off, which means the comb is very easy to lift out.

Cons

- Old brood combs can be difficult to cull.

6: The hex hive

The hex hive has a special design to give your bees as much of a natural environment as possible. The design even mimics a tree hollow, and the hexagonal shape imitates the cell shape of the bees, thus providing a familiar face. On top of that, the foundationless frame allows the bees to build their comb.

Willow Hankinson built this hexagonal shape design in Australia. The hex hive uses both top bars and three-sided frames to fill in the gaps.

Pros

- It is eco-friendly because the hive uses reclaimed material.

- It allows the bees to create natural combs.

- It facilitates the free flow of air due to the hexagonal shape that eliminates the cold spots.

- It allows for the extraction of honey using a centrifugal extractor.

Cons

- The design allows pests to hide.

- Full boxes are heavy to move or lift.

- Not easily accessible since you have to remove the roof.

- The wax combs can easily absorb pesticides and metal.

Those are the most common beehives you'll find around. You should pick the one that best suits your needs.

If you don't want to buy a readymade beehive and have great woodworking skills, you can build a hive.

How to Build Your Beehive

Most of the beehives we have discussed are not easy to get, and some might not meet your needs. Therefore, the best thing to do is build a beehive that meets your exact needs and is perfectly efficient.

Building a beehive might seem difficult, but it is easier than you think. All you need are the right tools and the right guidance to create a great standard beehive.

The design we're going to build is a Langstroth hive, the most commonly used, and that you can customize based on the size of your colony. You can always keep adding and building depending on how many bees you have.

The idea is to revert to the industrialized way of obtaining honey that involves 10,000 and 30,000 bees.

Tools required

- Drill
- Dado
- Tin snips
- Miter saw
- Table saw

Materials required

- 10 board
- 1 by 2 board

- 1-½" trim head screws
- ¼" plywood
- 2" trim head screws
- 1 by 3 board

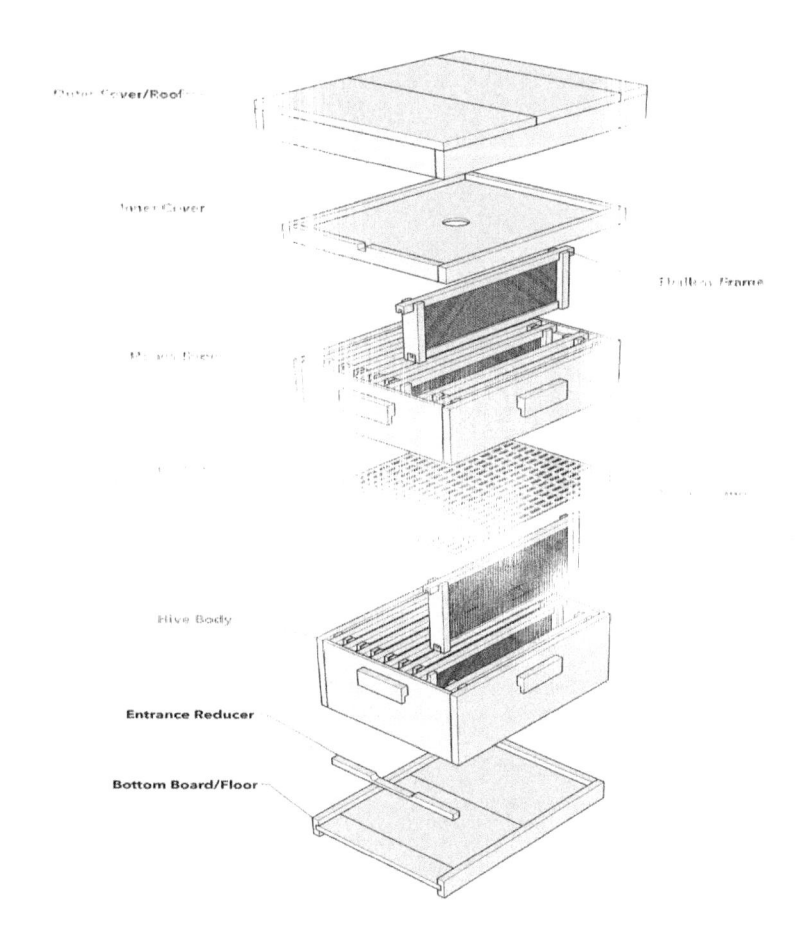

Cutting list

Key	Qty	Material	Dimensions	Part
Bottom Board/Floor				
A	2	1x3 board	3/4" x 2-1/2" x 22"	Sides
B	1	1x3 board	3/4" x 2-1/2" x 2"	Back
C	2	1x10 board	3/4" x 9-1/4" x 15-1/4"	Floor board
D	1	1x10 board	3/4" x 2-3/4"* x 15-1/4"	Floor board
Entrance Reducer				
E	1	1x3 board	3/4" x 7/8" x 14-1/2"	Entrance reducer
Hive Body				
F	2	1x10 board	3/4" x 9-1/4" x 14-1/2"	Ends
G	2	1x10 board	3/4" x 9-1/4" x 19-3/4"	Sides
H	4	1x3 board	3/4" x 2-1/2" x 5"	Handles
Honey Super				
J	2	1x10 board	3/4" x 6" x 14-1/2"	Ends
K	2	1x10 board	3/4" x 6" x 19-3/4"	Sides
L	4	1x3 board	3/4" x 2-1/2" x 5"	Handles
Frame (Qty based on one frame)				
M	1	1x2 board	3/4" x 3/4" x 19"	Top bar
N	2	1x2 board	3/4" x 1-1/4" x 8-1/2"	End bars
P	1	1x2 board	3/4" x 3/4" x 17"	Bottom bar
Inner Cover				
Q	2	1x2 board	3/4" x 1-1/2" x 19-3/4"	Sides
R	2	1x2 board	3/4" x 1-1/2" x 14-1/2"	Ends
S	1	1/4" plywood	1/4" x 14-1/2" x 19"	Center board
Outer Cover/Roof				
T	2	1x3 board	3/4" x 2-1/2" x 21-7/8"	Sides
U	2	1x3 board	3/4" x 2-1/2" x 16-1/4"	Ends
V	2	1x10 board	3/4" x 9-1/4" x 17-3/4"	Top board
W	1	1x10 board	3/4" x 3"* x 17-3/4"	Top board
X	1	Aluminum	Cut to fit	Aluminum top

*Scribe and cut to fit

The project plans

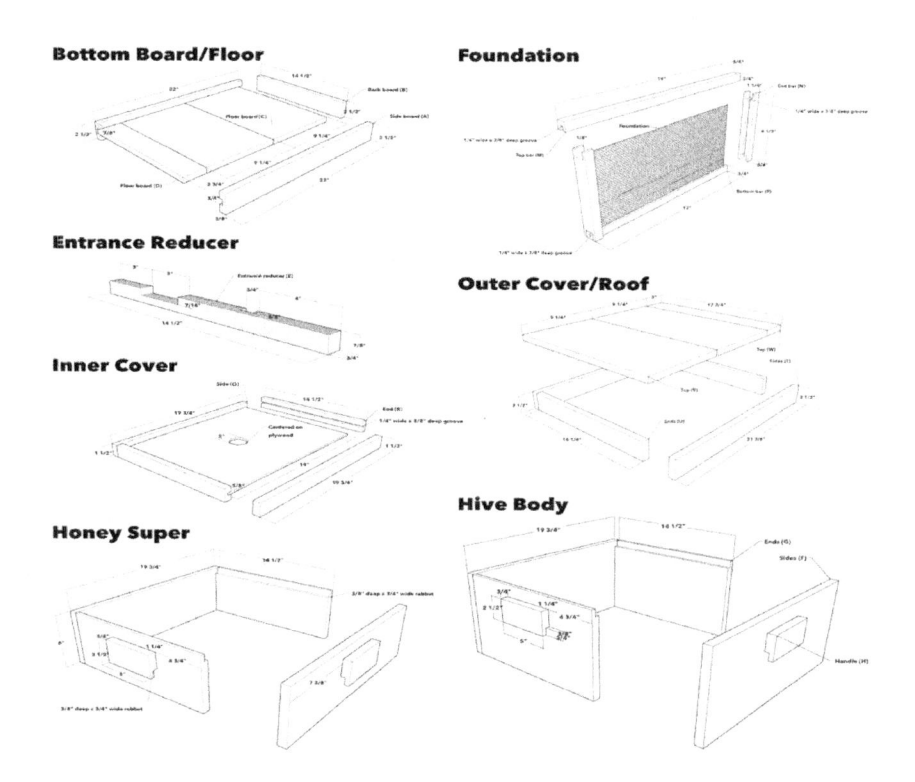

Bottom Board/Floor

Foundation

Entrance Reducer

Outer Cover/Roof

Inner Cover

Honey Super

Hive Body

Procedure

1. Start by cutting A-D using the miter saw, then center a ¾" by ⅜" deep dado into side A. Next, fasten side B with glue and 2" trim head screws.

2. Place the two one by ten floorboards into place, then place the final floorboard into place before ripping the board into the scribbled width of the table saw. Next, glue and screw the floorboards into the right place.

3. Now crosscut the 1" by 3" to 14 ½", rip it to ⅞" using the table saw, then set up your dado stack to cut ¾" by ⅜" deep notch.

4. Next, cut a 3" wide notch at the entrance reducer, 3" from one end. Next, rotate the entrance by 90°, then make one pass 4" from the other end.

5. Crosscut the parts again to length before cutting a 3/8" by ¾" into the edge of a wide rabbet using a sacrificial fence. Fasten the sides of the body hive using glue and screws.

6. Now cut a ⅜" by a ¾" wide rabbet into a 22" using a table saw before crosscutting the four 5" long handles out of the 1 by 3.

7. Try and center the handles on each body on each face about 1¼" from the rabbeted edge, then fasten it in place using glue and screws.

8. To create the frames, cut a ½" into two ¾" then crosscut them to 19" before ripping and crosscutting a 1 by 2 into a 1 1/4" by 8 ½." Cut a ¾" by ¾" notch into the center of each board.

9. Now cut a ¼" by ⅜" groove into the center of each part to create the top bar. Next, slowly place the

beeswax foundation under the frame of the bottom bar before drilling pilot holes from the end bars and into the top or bottom bars.

10. The next thing is to crosscut the 1 by 2 to length before cutting a ¼" by ⅜" dado into the center of the 14 ½" ends. Now cut a ¾" by ⅜" deep notch on the center of one of the 14 ½". Crosscut and rip the ¼" plywood to the required size for the centerboard.

11. Take the aluminum and cut with tin snips to 2" longer and wider than the box before placing the wood at the center of the outline of the assembly and center of the aluminum. Glue the aluminum to the surface using construction adhesive until it sticks properly.

12. For a smooth corner, hammer the edges of the aluminum using a mallet.

That is just about everything you need to know about beehives and how to construct the perfect one for you that suits your needs. The next thing to learn is getting the right bees for you.

Chapter 4

The Right Bees For You

Once you get the perfect beehive for you, the next step is to find the best bees that will bring you enough produce.

Bees might look the same, but different types of bees are available, each with a specific set of characteristics and benefits. Therefore, it is important to figure out the perfect bees for you to look after.

As a beginner, it can be tricky to figure out where to get the bees, which strain or race to order, and what to do when getting the bees. Luckily, this chapter will discuss this extensively.

To get started, here is a list of the most common bee species you can buy.

The Most Common Bee Species

The most common bee species are:

Italian Bees

This kind of bee is the most popular race in the United States. First introduced in 1859, these bees replaced the original black or German bee brought by colonialists.

The Italian bee is usually brown or light yellowish and tends to have alternating stripes of black and brown on its abdomen. Those that have three abdominal bands or five bands are known as leather-colored Italians and golden, respectively.

The Italian bee species usually starts brood-rearing in the spring and continues till late fall, which causes a large population during the entire active season. Also, most of the Italian bee strains are gentle and quiet on the combs. Since the Italian bees are usually many, they can quickly collect a considerable amount of nectar, which means more honey; however, they also require equally as much during winter.

The disadvantages of the Italian bees are that they have a weaker orientation than other races, which causes them to move from one colony to another, increasing their chances of contracting diseases.

However, they are considered great housekeepers, and the lighter color of the Italian queen makes it easier to spot her than is the case with other races. In addition, these bees are popular for producing great white capping that is useful for producing comb and honey.

Carnolians

This species usually has dark bees that are almost similar in appearance to the Caucasian except that they have brown spots or bands on their abdomen. Carolinas usually go through winter in small clusters and only start to increase rapidly when the first pollen becomes available in spring.

As a result, the major issue with this species is excessive swarming due to the rapidly increasing number of bees. The good thing is that during winter, the bees cluster in small numbers, making this species very economical regarding food consumption during winter.

They also don't move from one colony to another, which means they are well oriented and usually quiet on the honeycombs. They are usually available but are by no means common. Sometimes their stock is usually referred to as new World Carnolians and is considered the better version by some beekeepers.

Buckfast bees

The buck fast bee species is a hybrid product selected over a long time from a selection of many strains of bees from Southwestern England.

Studies have shown that the Buckfast bees are usually resistant to tracheal mites and are better suited for cool climates. Fortunately, these bees are easy to find because the US often imports Buckfast bee colonies.

Hybrid bees

The hybrid species is a combination of several lines or races of honey bees. Planned crosses result in a line of very prolific bees that portray something called hybrid vigor.

The best way to control hybrid vigor is mating. Commercial hybrids are usually a result of a combination of crisscrossing inbred lines developed and maintained for certain characteristics such as productivity, wintering, and gentleness.

Other Species

Aside from these well-known species, we have other species that have been developed for drug-resistant diseases as well as destrustive parasites like mites.

Some of these species include the West Virginia selection, the buckeye strain from Ohio, and breeder queens from Buck fast Abbey in England. These bees have shown great results in terms of resisting tracheal mites. They have also been seen to have many other superior traits.

If you happen to use bees of a selected stock or hybrid bees in your hives, you will need to requeen regularly. Failing to replace the queen by allowing the natural process to take place tends to result to a loss of hybrid vigor; sometimes, it can make colonies to be difficult to manage – like being too aggressive/defensive.

How to Choose The Best Location For Your Bees

Before you can go ahead and bring the bees to the beehive in your backyard, you need to make sure the location is great. While bees can thrive just about anywhere, finding the perfect spot can make a great deal of difference.

Below are certain criteria you can use to find the best area for your hive.

#: *Access to plenty of water*

Bees are usually very resourceful creatures when it comes to the growth of their colony. And for their colony to grow, the bees usually head out to look for water to help them cool their hives and to thin out honey for eating.

Therefore, bees have this uncanny ability to find natural water sources, some of which you might not even know existed. However, to keep your bees from using polluted water, you can try setting up clean water near the hives so that you can eliminate the chances of your bees going astray.

In other cases, some beekeepers usually have small water gardens that the bees can enjoy.

#: *Flowers for your bees*

Common sense dictates that bees get the pollen they need to make honey from the flowers near their hive. Therefore, you can help make sure that they create quality honey by planting flowers around your backyard.

Bees generally love flowers with tubular flowers with nectar at the base and a good landing platform. Flowers such as dandelions, snapdragons, and daises are great additions to your yard because they produce great pollen and nectar.

Bees are also attracted to yellow and blue flowers the most. Therefore, having either of the flowers with such colors makes it more visible to the bees.

Also, bees love flowers with flower spikes since it allows the bees to move from one flower to another quickly. These are flowers like catnip, goldenrod, and sage.

#: *Around trees and shrubs to help provide nectar and pollen*

During the early season, trees and shrubs can provide a flush of pollen and nectar before any other plant starts to emerge. Unlike grass lawns that provide no shelter and no food for the bees, trees and shrubs offer shelter and food. This, together with some flowering plants, will benefit you in many ways as a beekeeper.

Early season bee nectar plants

- **Perennials:** bugloss, pig squeak, viola, blueberries, crocus, and lungwort.

- **Trees:** apples, plums, honeysuckles, maples, cherries, and shadbush.

Mid-season bee nectar plants

- **Perennials:** purple coneflowers, mint, milkweed, bee balm, blazing star, and Oregon.

- **Annuals:** borage, single-flowered marigold, blanket flower, and tickseed.

- **Shrubs:** rosebay, spirea, rhododendron, and summer sweet.

Late season bee nectar plants

- **Annuals:** snapdragon and cosmos.

- **Perennials:** goldenrod, aster, yellow and purple coneflower, and bottle gentian.

#: Enough space around the hive

As you know already, honey bees can forage for several miles around the hive, looking for pollen, nectar, and other hive needs. Sometimes, you'll find that the beehive entrance appears congested with bee traffic, and while some bees don't mind sharing the yard with people, some can be very protective.

Therefore, this means that if the bees happen to feel congested or threatened by people, they'll retaliate by stinging. Therefore, to avoid putting yourself, your family, and your pet in such a situation, ensure your bees have enough space in your yard or away from people. A privacy fence is a good idea if you're working with limited space because it screens access.

The biggest danger zone is usually the beehive entrance, making it important to ensure you don't place the hive entrance close to walkways or near people.

#: Easily accessible area

As much as you need to give your bees enough space to do their business, the area you decide to keep them should be easily accessible. After all, you still need to observe and see how your hive is progressing.

Having an accessible hive also allows you to know if something happens to your hive before it is too late. Additionally, access means you can see the areas lacking and do something to enhance the bees' living conditions.

Thus, ensure that the location you choose allows for easy and periodic observation. You'll even get to know or learn about the nature of the bees you have.

#: *Place the beehive at a height*

Whether you use a stand for your hive or you hang the beehive on a tree, make sure to raise the beehive off the ground.

The main reason for this is that placing your hive at a height will help protect it from predators, and you won't have to keep bending as you tend to the hive. The recommended height is usually about 18 inches from the ground, but how high you decide to place it is a personal choice.

Also, raising the hive reduces the moisture effect and facilitates free airflow. As you very well know, ventilation is crucial to the health of your colony. The life of the hive will also improve when you place it off the ground.

Those are some of the important factors you need to keep in mind while choosing the best location for your hive or bees.

With all these characteristics in play, you can attract most bee species.

Where to Get Bees

Now that you have a great hive and the perfect location, the next thing to do is get the bees for your hive. For a beginner, the easiest and safest way to start an apiary is to buy the bees. However, there are two main ways to get bees:

1: Package bees

To get packaged bees, you can contact your local beekeeper supplier or local beekeeping association. Packaged bees usually consist of a queen, multiple workers, and a feeder filled with syrup.

To handle this bee package well, your supplier should provide adequate information on how to successfully install the package in their new home and ways to introduce the queen to the workers.

The most common way to introduce the queen to the workers is using the indirect method comprised of the f workers eating their way through the food plug as they familiarize themselves with the queen.

2: Nucleus hive

Another option is to get a nucleus hive made up of a half-sized colony; the most common is a five-frame nuc.

A five-frame nuc means you're getting five frames of comb, a queen, honey, bees, and brood. By getting a nuc, you gain an advantage because it gives you an edge over colony growth.

However, this approach comes with the risk of pests and diseases from the original hive to your hive.

Make sure to consult with your local beekeeping association on the best place to buy healthy bees in your region.

Getting Bees in The Wild

The cluster of bees you occasionally see in the wild is known as a swarm; it results from overcrowding. When a beehive has bees at a rate that threatens survival, the colony usually divides given that the growing colony requires more room to keep up with the growth.

Swarming is a natural bee tendency that occurs more often the spring. Catching a swarm isn't that difficult because the bees are already willing to get a new home, and thus, they are usually mild-mannered.

Regardless, make sure to wear protective clothing and, if possible, carry sugar water syrup and a smoker to calm down any violent bees.

Bees found on a fence post or flat surface are easy to guide into a container. All you will need to do is to use a piece of cardboard to brush them gently, just like you would do with a dustpan. Another strategy is to puff smoke behind them so that you can guide them to move in the opposite direction.

You can collect bees found in limbs by cutting the limb and gently shaking it inside a container. The same concept applies to transferring the bees from the container to your beehive; gently shake the container towards a prepared beehive.

However, getting bees from the wild comes with the risk of carrying diseases or having a weak genetic material. The queen might even be hurt or killed, which is usually difficult to identify among wild bees.

In addition, just because you've seen wild bees doesn't mean that you can take them because some states have laws governing property rights. For example, if the tree limb is in your neighbor's yard, it would be considered stealing if you take those bees. To avoid this, check with your local ordinance the laws governing what you'd like to do.

You can choose whichever convenient way of getting bees. For example, if you have a bee association in your area, then they might guide you on the best way to get your bees.

The Best Time To Get Your Bees

Before you can go ahead and get the bees for your hive, it is important to find out the best season to do so.

This is important because it can increase your chances of success and so that you can kick start on a high note.

The best time to start beekeeping is spring when the weather begins to warm up, and the flowers start to blossom. Once this season arrives, get your bees into the hive as fast as you can so that they can start preparing the hive before fall rolls in. By then, your hive should have established, and honey should be in plenty to avoid any unforeseen complications.

If you're ordering bees online, make sure they are delivered exactly at the beginning of the spring season, not before or after.

Number of Bees Required to Start a Hive

If you decide to buy package bees, you'll need a swarm of about 10,000 bees and one mated queen. That translates to about 2.5 to 3 pounds because a single bee usually weighs about 0.00025 to 0.00030 pounds.

For an old hive that already is producing honey, you can get about 50,000+ bees that weigh about 12+ pounds to get started.

Make sure to get bees of all age classes because they need to do different jobs in the hive. With a mated queen and other bees (drones and workers) of all sizes, you'll be good to go.

The average hobbyist should start beekeeping with two or more beehives because, with two hives, you can compare things and have a backup plan. By having two hives, you'll replace a queen in case of anything. You can take the brood from one hive and place it on the other that is queen-less. Also, if one colony gets weak, simply add more bees to equalize. Therefore, having two hives makes managing them a lot easier.

With this information at hand, you're in a good position to pick the right bees for you, when to do so and how to bring them into your hive.

Now let's look at what you need to do in preparation for the bees in your hive.

Bringing The Bees Home

Once you've gotten the bees for your hive, that's where the real jobs begin. Creating a conducive environment and preparing yourself to receive the bees is crucial; it helps you avoid making costly mistakes. Therefore, in this chapter, we'll discuss how to welcome and accommodate the bees the right way.

How Packaged Bees Travel

As a beginner, you're probably curious about transporting bees from one point to the other. Well, transporting packaged bees usually sees the queen transported separately from the other bees.

The bees you purchase will travel from their original location to yours in special wooden boxes with screened sides for ventilation. That is particularly important to help make sure that the bees don't overheat during the transportation process. Inside the big box, there is a much smaller box with one screened side that contains the queen.

Normally, inside the box, the suppliers usually suspend a can of syrup with a hole that is enough for the bees to access but not big enough to spill during transit. The bees will feed on this syrup during the entire period as they also feed the queen in her small box.

Preparing for the Bees

To avoid making mistakes and ensure that you take care of your bees the right way, you need to do several preparative things.

The syrup the bees will be feasting on during the travel will most likely be finished or near to finish by the time it gets to you. That's why it is important to start feeding the bees as soon as they arrive.

You can prepare syrup for them by combining equal portions of sugar and water then boiling until the sugar dissolves completely. When the bees first get to your home, bring them to a safe location while still in the box, then spray the sugar syrup on the screen. Keep the bees in the box for about a week with constant feeding as you prepare your hive.

By this time, you should have found the best location for your hive according to previously discussed characteristics. Ensure your hive location does not tilt or slant because bees hate that. If it so happens to be slanted, take your time and shim the hive to ensure its level.

Putting the Bees into the Beehive

After getting acquainted with your bees, the next step is to bring them into the beehive without making a mistake. Doing this may seem like a daunting challenge, but it can be quite easy if done the right way.

When you finally get ready to move the bees into the hive, bring the package of bees out to the beehive. Next, remove the outer lid and the inner cover before removing 3 or 4 frames from the top super. Keep those frames aside for the time being.

Take the package of bees and shake it properly so that it pushes the bees to the bottom. Then, quickly remove the lid and invert the package over the top of the open hive to release the bees out.

The bees will fall into the hive and continue with their normal business. However, if some begin buzzing around, keep your moves deliberate and methodical. Doing that should stop them from bothering you. However, make sure you're wearing your protective gear as you deal with them.

After successfully removing all the bees, the next step is to remove the queen from the small box. Slowly replace the frames you removed earlier than release the queen between two frames. Finally, replace the hive inner cover and lid to complete the process.

If, for any reason, there may be an issue with the flowers being in bloom and producing pollen, consider giving your bees supplemental food until they are efficient enough to forage for themselves.

The best way to feed your bees is using a hive top feeder. This feeder offers a small platform for syrup placement. The feeder's lid should have small holes that allow the bees to access the food, or you can puncture the holes using the tip of the nail.

However, make sure that the holes are not big enough to pour the syrup. Also, puncture the lids from the outside so that any metal points face away and inwards from the bees.

Place the feeder in a frameless super, then place the hive's lid and inner cover. Once done implementing all that, you are good to go.

That is the procedure you need to follow when you get your bees and install them in their new home. The next thing you need to learn is how to monitor them and what to do when a situation arises when dealing with them.

Chapter 5
Checking and Maintaining Your Bees

This is a crucial part of any beekeeping cycle because it determines whether or not your bees will survive. If you don't check up on your bees, especially during the first few weeks of establishing a colony, you run the risk of losing your colony. Therefore, it is important to keep tabs on your hive to ensure you can take action when doing so is in your best interest as a beekeeper. Although bees are self-sufficient creatures, they sometimes need help.

How Often To Tend To Your Bees

For a new hive, you need to plan for an inspection every week. Then, once everything has settled, you can do a routine check once a month, unless you suspect an issue.

It is essential to have a concrete inspection schedule. Unfortunately, there is no definite schedule that fits all hives because issues are different. For example, healthy hives don't need regular inspection, but other hives might need a weekly inspection to recover from parasites or diseases.

Here is a general schedule you can use to conduct inspections on your hive.

Late winter or spring (every 7-10 days)

During this period, you need to be on the lookout for any signs of swarming, which you can see through overcrowding or developing queen cells.

Figure out whether or not you need to split or combine your hive for the next season.

Late spring to late summer (every 3 to 4 weeks)

Conduct routine checkups to determine the health of your hive.

If the honey becomes plenty, you can increase the time between inspections and begin harvesting to allow the bees to make more.

Every fall to winter (No inspections)

During this period, please do not open the hive to check on their food supply. Instead, slowly lift the hive on one side to check the weight.

As a beginner, you might feel tempted to keep your hive open, which is wrong. Instead, it's in your best interest to keep the hive open as little as possible while still keeping track of the season's changes and activities. Over inspecting can compromise the integrity of your bees, even though it is important to inspect the frames for diseases.

Once you get used to it, you'll learn more about bees and be able to identify when something is not right quickly. At this point, you'll be able to notice abnormal aggressive behavior, their sound, dead bees around the hive, and fewer bees leaving the hive. You'll also know what to do to rectify things.

When Not to Open a Beehive

You cannot always open your hive for inspection. This is because the weather needs to be optimal. After all, if you open your hive when it's too cold, too hot, windy, or rainy, it will stress the bees.

Try and open your hive when the temperature outside is similar to the conditions inside the hive. One thing to note is that the weather needs to be warm without wind or rain.

What You Need for a Hive Inspection

Before you open your hive for inspection, there are several things you'll need to make the work easier. These things include:

#: Beekeeping suit

A beekeeping suit is the most important item any beekeeper needs for beekeeping because it protects you from bee stings. It's best to have a full suit from head to toe so that it can protect you from any attack that may arise.

The suit will give you the courage to inspect the hive without worrying too much about stings or an attack. Before inspecting a hive, ensure you have on a good quality suit.

#: Hive tool

The hive tool looks like a crowbar and helps pry open the boxes whenever you want to inspect your hive.

This tool is especially important when opening the box that might have stuck together due to beeswax. It also allows you to remove the combs from the side of the hive.

#: Smoker

A smoker is an essential tool that helps calm down irritable bees. It usually resembles a forest flower that prompts them to get ready for the next move.

The smoke also blocks the communication within the hive, thus minimizing the colony reaction. This helps to calm the bees as you continue with your inspections.

#: Bee brush

A bee brush is a useful tool used to remove the bees from the surface of the combs or any other unwanted places.

However, bees don't like the brushing motion and will try to sting it; thus, use the brush sparingly.

Routine Hive Inspection Procedure

Once your bees get established in their new home, they will have a lot of work to do. That includes populating the hives with more bees, storing food for winter, and building combs.

When conducting a routine inspection of your hive, there are certain things you need to be on the lookout for; these things include:

#: Brood pattern

You can start by checking on the brood nest to find out how your hive is reproducing. Ensure you check for brood nest development so

If you see eggs and larvae, then it means the colony has accepted the new queen. Also, check and see if the health of the brood pattern is good.

#: Queen check

As a new beekeeper, you'll need to see if the hive has accepted the queen and if she has assumed her rightful position.

You can know that the queen is alright and accepted when you see new eggs and larva. Once you confirm that she is okay, you don't need to check on her every time you conduct an inspection.

#: Pollen and honey

At the beginning of the season, you need to make sure that your bees keep bringing in pollen and nectar.

During summer, check and see if your supers are producing honey. If they aren't, that means there is no nectar in your area. You need to consider feeding your bees.

#: Signs of swarming

During spring, colonies have a higher chance of swarming, and so you should be on the look out for any signs. Check to see if queen cells are developing well or if the hive is overcrowded. Also, check the frames to see how many of them are covered with bees.

#: *Diseases and pests*

Diseases and pests are very problematic when it comes to the health of any colony. Mainly, this is because these pests and diseases can cause the health of your colony to deteriorate significantly, leading to huge losses.

Therefore, you need to check for any signs of pests and diseases in your hive. If you happen to spot any of them in your hive, you need to clean your hive, add traps or barriers, then give treatments to exterminate any threat.

Record Keeping for Beekeepers

To help you keep track of these inspections and all other things you need to record as a bee farmer, you'll need a journal. A journal will help you track how your beekeeping venture is going on, ensuring you don't forget anything you observe during your various inspections.

Importance of Bee Keeping Records

There are many advantages to keeping a record journal when you conduct your inspections. Those benefits include:

#: *Tracking the queen*

You need to ensure that the colony has accepted the queen and that she's performing has duties dutifully. The queen can sometimes be tricky to see, but the good thing is that there are things in the hive you can see to determine if she's okay.

These indicators include brood stages, brood patterns, and eggs; all can tell you how well your queen is doing. Keeping track of these things from one inspection to another can help you decide which activities you need to take to keep your hive healthy. Having a journal is particularly important if you have many hives; it makes it possible to keep records that will refresh your mind.

#: Gain knowledge

If you're looking for a great way to learn more about beekeeping in general and your bees in particular, then a journal would be great.

When you record your observations, you'll gain more details on bee behaviors, which will push you to do research. And as you become more experienced, you'll try out new techniques that will help you gain more insight into the beekeeping activity.

Keeping a record will help you learn what works for you and your apiary.

#: Identifying and monitoring diseases and infestation

When you keep good records of what is happening in your hive, it can help you know when your pests and diseases attack your bees. If you happen to see one small hive beetle in a colony, it is not a big deal. However, recording it will help you look for further signs of further infestation in the next inspection.

Find out if the bees are defensive when faced with danger. Tracking your bees' behavior during such invasions will help you decide what to do in terms of protecting your hive. In addition, it will help you decide

#: Track honey production

Keeping a record of how your bees produce honey will help you know if the bees you got are productive. If you find that the honey is not enough, you might consider feeding them or providing winter supplements.

Tracking is also a key part of ensuring that you give your bees enough nourishment for winter. You can also dictate if you're in a dearth when your bees start consuming honey instead of producing more.

#: To meet legal requirements

In some states, you might be legally obliged to engage in legal record-keeping as a requirement. For example, in Australia, the Biosecurity Code of Practice dictates that all beekeepers must keep records of:

- A record of the sampling and testing for the American foulbrood.
- The dates and observations from your various inspections, including any pests found and the strength of your hive.

- The details on the exact location and movements of your bees.

- The steps you've taken to control any pests or infestations.

- If you have employees, their training records, etc.

- Details on the supplier of your bees and your introduction process.

- At least three years of records.

- Records of your honey sales in your area.

In New York, the city requires all beekeepers to notify them 30 days after establishing the hive. Therefore, to register, you'll need:

- A detailed explanation of where the bees are (location-wise).

- A reminder of any necessary renewals.

- A record of when you set up your hive.

- The paperwork required for future filings.

#: Tracking finances

Beekeeping may start as a hobby, but with time, you might want to commercialize it. And when that happens, you'll need to keep financial recordings.

Records will help you monitor your profitability and report on income tax and sales. It is also worth recording the costs of establishing yourself as a beekeeper for future reference.

Records to Keep in Your Journal

As much as recording information is important, you need to know what exactly you should record. The starting point is the mandatory information required by law or regulations. Here is a detailed explanation of the specific things you need to record.

#: Equipment records

You need to keep a record of the things you have; that way, you can know if something is missing or when to get a new tool. These records include:

- The cost
- Inventory
- Supplies

#: *Apiary records*

This information is crucial in cases where you have to register in your locality. Even if you're not going to register, it is important to record this information. Apiary records include:

- The location
- The number of hives in each
- The number of apiaries

#: *Hive records*

You need to have records of each hive, especially if you have several to track each one individually. The information to record includes:

- Bees - the kind of bees (how they behave, the number, handle, produce, mites (e.t.c)
- Identifier - number - color - queen - name.
- Colony source
- Movements
- Queen information

#: *Harvest*

You need to make sure that your bees are as productive as possible. The best way to do this is by tracking how much produce you get from your bees. Keep a record of:

- Propolis
- Pollen
- Honey
- Queens reared
- Beeswax

#: *Inspection records*

Keeping records of your colony when you conduct your inspections will determine future tasks and reminders. For instance, it will help you to the things you need to address.

Here is the information you need:

- Weather
- Dates
- Temperament and behavior of the bees
- Population

- Queen status

- Feeding

- Stores

- Presence and number of swarm cells

- Infestation

- Weight

- Chemicals used for treatment

- Action for the next inspection.

#: *Financial records*

As you get into beekeeping, you might want to track your expenditures and earnings. Financial records can help you manage and understand your business. This information includes:

- Tax payments and filings

- Detailed income and expenses

- Banking records

- Form and structure of ownership

- Banking records

- Accounts payables and receivables
- Customer listing and orders

Record keeping is the best way to learn about your bees and manage your colonies.

How to Deal with a Bee Sting

If you get stung by a bee, it can cause some very adverse effects. You may end up experiencing sharp pain, warmth, redness, swelling, and itching at the area affected, but nothing serious.

However, if you happen to be allergic to bee stings, then getting stung can be life-threatening. Some of the symptoms of a severe allergic reaction to a bee sting include dizziness, severe itching, swelling of your tongue and throat, hives, pale skin, rapid pulse, loss of consciousness, and difficulty breathing.

When a bee stings you, it usually leaves behind a toxin that causes you to experience those symptoms.

The interesting fact is that when a bee stings you, it dies shortly after. Thus, honey bees are the only types of bees that die after stinging someone.

Home Remedies For A Bee Sting

Unless you're highly allergic to bee stings, you can treat most of the bee stings at home.

After getting stung by a bee, the first thing you should do is remove the stinger immediately, which you can do using your fingertips. Doing this curbs the toxins entering your body.

Now thoroughly wash the area affected using water and soap. To reduce the itching or swelling, you can try placing ice on the affected area.

Some home remedies to help alleviate the symptoms of a bee sting include:

- Applying honey to the affected area, then covering with a loose bandage for up to an hour.

- Smear toothpaste to the affected area.

- Soak the affected area in a container of diluted apple cider vinegar for 15 minutes.

- Apply a solution of meat tenderizer and water to the affected area for 30 minutes.

- Apply a wet aspirin or aspirin paste to the affected area to reduce the pain and swelling.

- Use herbs and oils on the affected area; some oils and herbs you can use include lavender, aloe vera, witch hazel, calendula cream, and tea tree oil.

When To See A Doctor

Most bee stings will not require you to see a doctor. However, it is best to see a doctor in special situations such as multiple stings or a serious allergic reaction. Contact your local health provider immediately you get into such a situation or call for help. Try using your EpiPen first, then visit a doctor as soon as possible.

The bottom line is that bee stings can be quite painful and very uncomfortable. Thus, it would be best to take precautions to avoid getting stung. Aside from wearing protective clothing as you deal with your bees, other protective measures you can put in place include:

- Stay away from beehives as much as possible.
- Avoid wearing bright colors near bees.
- Avoid drinking open soda cans.
- Don't put on sweet-smelling perfume.
- Avoid walking barefoot outside.

- Keep away from uncovered garbage cans.

- Always cover your food.

Just take care not to provoke the bees as you work with them. It is always better to be safe than sorry. With that in mind, the next step is to understand bee behavior during the seasons.

Chapter 6

Bees Throughout The Seasons

As a new beekeeper, worrying about the future and the many things that can go wrong can be draining. This apprehension worsens when you probably won't know how exactly things will unfold. Fortunately, knowing what to expect can change that.

For starters, knowing what to expect would help you understand and manage your hive. Additionally, knowing how bees behave during the various seasons can help you know when something goes wrong or if you're on the right track.

Here is how bees behave during spring, summer, autumn, and winter.

Spring

During winter, the queen usually lays many eggs each day. Therefore, by the first time you conduct your inspection as a new beekeeper, you'll find that the brood will be enormous.

The forage is very important here because many young bees need feeding and the elderly remaining workforce needs replacing.

The days will most likely be sunny and mild, which means that the bees can move around much easier. And so, when the bees are free to move, it means that the colony will expand rapidly and possibly outgrow the hive. This state will push the bees to look for some extra room through a process called swarming.

During this swarming process, the bees usually start to raise a new queen and slim the old queen in preparation to fly. Once the new queen is on the way for sure, the old queen will leave the hive with other workers. Normally, the swarm will land close by as the workers look for a new home.

And while swarms might look very scary and dangerous, they are usually very peaceful because they don't have a home or young to feed.

Winter

During the winter solstice, there is usually little to no sign of activity. Sometimes the hive will even look abandoned. During this season, bees depend on the honey they've created to consume as they winter out the entire season.

As soon as the sun comes out, it will trigger a change inside the hive. The worker bees usually start feeding the queen a little more food, which triggers her to start laying more eggs.

If the temperatures happen to be high enough during winter, the bees will fly and collect water for diluting the honey. Also, the bees will try collecting pollen if any is available since it is essential for rearing a strong, healthy brood.

Autumn

In summer, bees only live for approximately six weeks; comparatively, the workers can live up to six months in winter. Therefore, the bees produced during this season are especially required to be healthy and strong since they'll be the ones to keep the colony going during winter.

Also, bees hatched in this period are responsible for starting the beehives afresh when they are very elderly and almost dead. About 10,000 bees are required to keep the colony up and running during winter because as the days go by, the colony reduces in size as the old bees die.

The bees continue to forage until the last day when it gets frigid, and they have to form a cluster. The queen is usually in the middle of that cluster together with the brood to keep them warm. The worker bees usually flap their wings to generate heat for the entire cluster.

That is where the cycle ends before it begins again in winter.

Summer

Once summer sets in after spring, the queen starts laying eggs profusely, which means that the young bees need feeding. Therefore, the worker bees continue to forage from dust to dawn to get the necessary food.

In this season, the colony can grow as big as 60,000 bees. Moreover, the summer solstice season usually affects general bee behavior. They do this by reducing the food they give to their queen, which means her laying eggs capacity reduces significantly.

This works out well because when the main nectar flow happens in late July to early August, more adult bees are available to forage.

Also, since there will be no considerable number of young bees to feed, the surplus nectar will be stored as honey as the bees prepare for winter.

Those are the four main seasons that occur each year, and with each one of them comes a different bee behavior. At least now you'll know what to expect or how to go about the various situations.

Chapter 7
All About Honey

After working tirelessly to make sure that your bees are home and your hive is up and running, you'll be ready to collect honey, which is one of the best parts of being a beekeeper.

As long as you've done everything right, you should expect a bountiful harvest of quality honey. And so, in this chapter, we will discuss everything you need to know about honey, including its benefits and how to harvest it.

Let's start by defining honey.

What is Honey?

Honey is usually many things to different people. However, many people define it as a nutritious, natural sweetener, ancient remedy, and energy source. Honey is also an active ingredient in skincare and beauty products and a subject of medical research.

How honey forms

When nectar, a sugary liquid, is extracted by the bees from flowers using their long, tube-like tongue, it gets stored in an extra stomach. As the nectar sloshes around the bee's stomach, its pH and composition after mixing with the enzymes changes causing it to last longer.

Once the bee gets back to the hive, it passes on the nectar to a different bee by regurgitating the nectar into its mouth. This process continues until the partially digested nectar gets finally deposited into the honeycomb.

The nectar at this point is a viscous liquid, nothing like what you see in honey. And so, to remove all the water from the honey, the bees use their wings to fan the honeycomb to help speed up the process.

When all the water evaporates from the honeycomb, the bees secrete a liquid from their abdomen that eventually hardens into beeswax then use it to seal the honeycombs. This process leads to the formation of honey.

How Honey Gets its Flavor, Color, and Fragrance

The taste and color of honey are usually affected by the type of flower providing the nectar and weather conditions in the various regions.

Amber-colored honey (such as avocados, blossom, orange, and eucalyptus) are moderately flavored, and light-colored honey (such as tupelo, alfalfa, and clover) are generally milder in flavor. The more deeply colored the honey is, the most intense flavor it has.

Several types of honey have different characteristics because of their different production method. They include orange blossom, clover, buckwheat, sage, dandelion, firewood, heather, macadamia nut, eucalyptus, palmetto, Manuka, blueberry, and avocado honey.

How Many Bees Does It Take To Make Honey?

Are you curious about exactly how many bees it takes to create honey? The rough estimate number of bees required to make a jar of honey is about 1152.

If one bee produces 1/12 of a teaspoon of honey, it takes around 12 bees to create a full teaspoon of honey. That automatically means that 36 bees can produce one tablespoon of honey. Therefore, to fill a 16 oz jar, you'll need 1152 bees.

An entire colony can produce anywhere from 60 to 100 pounds of honey each year.

How Often Can You Harvest Your Honey?

Harvesting is one of the most fun and rewarding parts of beekeeping. However, knowing how to harvest your honey and how often to do it can be tricky, especially for a beginner.

There are several things to consider when planning your honey harvest.

The first thing to consider is harvesting too early because you won't capitalize on the full amount. Also, you can't risk harvesting too late because you'll run the risk of getting into the cold weather, and taking honey might not leave enough for the bees.

In addition, you need to time when you treat your colony for pests and diseases to ensure it does not overlap with the honey flow period.

If this is your first year as a beekeeper with a new colony, you probably won't harvest all that much honey.

Most beekeepers usually harvest at least 2 to 3 times a season between the months of mid-June and mid-September. In rare cases, beekeepers can only harvest once per season, usually in early fall or late summer.

Honey Harvesting Equipment

To make the honey extraction process a lot easier, you'll need some equipment to help you through it. Aside from your suit and a smoker, other tools specific to the extraction process include:

#: A honey extractor

This tool uses centrifugal forces to squeeze the honey from the combs. Such tools usually come in many designs and sizes to fit any budget and need. However, for maximum efficiency, you need an extractor that can take at least four frames at a time.

#: *Honey strainer*

Before you can bottle your honey, you'll need to strain it first using this tool. This tool is similar to a sieve because it helps remove all the small particles such as bits of wax, wood, or any other thing.

#: *Honey uncapping knife*

An uncapping knife is what you'll use when you need to slice through wax cappings on a honeycomb quickly and cleanly. Bees usually create cappings on the honeycomb to protect the honey from air and water, but overtly, they make harvesting the honey challenging, which is there this tool comes in handy.

With this uncapping knife, you'll remove the cappings to extract the honey.

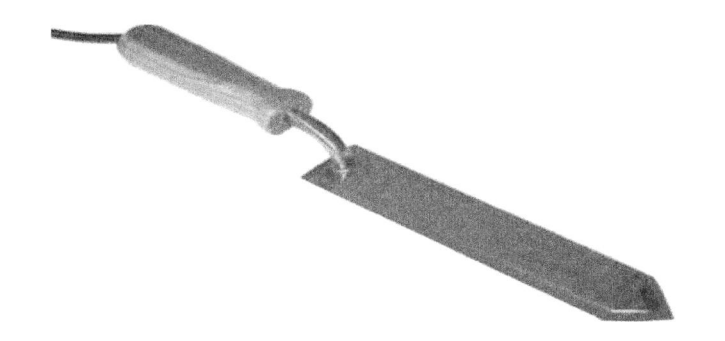

#: Double uncapping tank

This device is handy when collecting wax cappings once you slice them off the honeycombs. It allows you to extract the honey and the wax combs at the same time but separately.

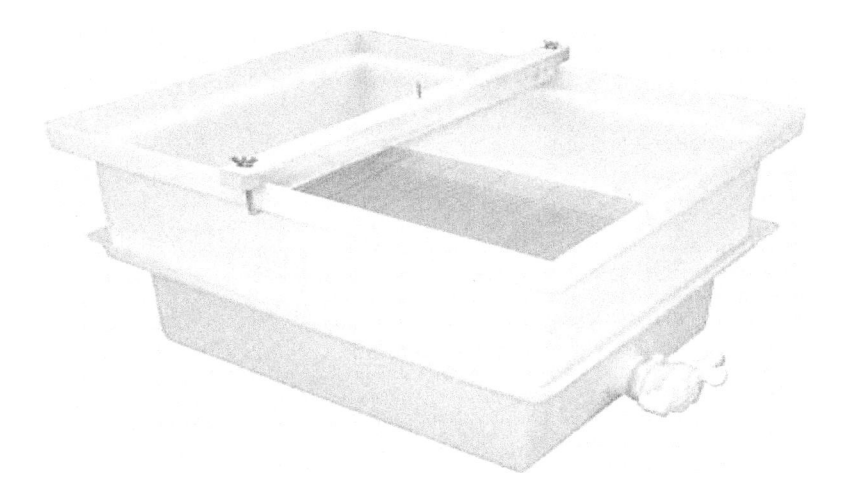

#: Honey uncapping fork

The honey fork helps remove the cappings off the honeycomb. Its main use is as a substitute or supplement to the uncapping knife. It especially helps open the stubborn cells that the uncapping knife might have left.

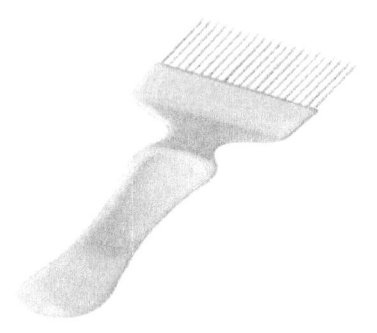

#: Bee brush

This tool helps clear the bees from the frame before their placement into the extractor. The ideal way to do this is by turning the frames upside down then brush the frames upside down before brushing. This ensures the bees drop off easily with no losses.

#: Honey bottling bucket

To make sure that your honey is safe and well protected, you'll need this tool. Honey bottling buckets are normally made of food-grade plastic and have a honey-dispensing tap at the bottom. Each bucket can hold up to 60 pounds of honey.

These are some of the most important tools you need when extracting honey. With those tools in place, you can go ahead and begin the extraction process.

How to Extract Honey From The Hive

When it comes time to harvest your honey, it is important to prepare yourself adequately to ensure you do the process the right way.

The first thing you should do is to get your proper clothing and equipment ready. Once ready, as you approach the hive, make gentle and calm movements. Do not try to rush the honey extraction process. Also, make sure that you're not wearing any perfumes, aftershave, or colognes.

Once you have your protective clothing on, the next step is to remove the bees from your hive. Doing this gives you easy access to the supers, which makes it easy to extract the honey.

There are several ways to move bees out of the super. These ways include:

- **Blowing the bees out of the super:** If you happen to have an air compressor, you can use it to blow off all the bees from the hive so that you can access the supers. If you don't have an air compressor, then you can use a leaf blower. However, this method is not all that effective at completely keeping bees away.

- **Brush the bees off the frames:** You can use a small light brush to brush the bees off the surface of the frames. Even though the bees won't like it, it is a great way to get rid of them.

- **Fume boards:** Another common method you can use to chase the bees away is using a fume board. A fume board is usually a little fabric with a strong, pungently smelling chemical poured on it. The chemical can be either Benzaldehyde or butyric acid. The foul smell from these chemicals usually chases the bees because they can't stand it, giving you enough room to take the frames out. Chasing the bees away like this gives you enough time to get what you need and return the frames to their right place.

- **Use bee escapes:** This is a tool used to allow the bees to exit but not re-enter. The three most common bee escapes include the triangle, conical, and porter escape.

Beekeepers usually place the triangle bee escape under the honey super, allowing bees to exit but cannot find their way back through the maze.

However, be advised that once this device removes all the bees from your supers, meaning the small hive beetle will have full reign over your hive. Thus, if your hive is in an area with a well-established history of SHB, you might consider using it sparingly or chose another option.

- **Smoker:** Lighting a smoker to release fumes into the hive causes the bees to be somewhat dormant. The fumes interfere with communication and visibility, allowing you to remove the bee frames.

How to Extract the Honey

After removing the bees from the hive, you should bring the frames to an area protected from the bees. Once you're in a safe area, you can begin the extraction process.

- You can use a manual or electric honey extractor to remove the honey. The machine uses centrifugal forces to separate the honey from the comb without destroying the comb, allowing you to use the empty frame back in the honey super.

- You can also use a hot knife to cut the wax cappings off the cells of the comb. Do not throw or destroy the wax cappings because you can use them to make candles. Once the cappings are out of the way, you can begin separating the liquid from the comb.

- Another option is to cut the honey-filled comb out of the frame. Then, using a cheesecloth, crush and strain the comb through it to separate the honey and the cappings.

- After extraction, let the honey sit for a few hours, then you can sieve to remove any unwanted particles.

Once done, the honey and beeswax are ready for us. Here are some of the common uses of honey and beeswax.

Benefits of Honey and Honeycomb

Many people have considered honey a popular kitchen staple and natural sweetener due to its medicinal and nutritional properties. Moreover, different cultures have used honey and honeycombs for different purposes.

Some of the benefits of these byproducts of keeping bees are:

- **Healing wounds:** Honey is usually considered an antibiotic that can work externally. Therefore, it's usable to treat wounds and sores by disinfecting them from any kind of bacteria.

- **Relieving the common cold:** Honey is known to have powerful anti-inflammatory properties that calm the irritable membrane that causes you to cough. Therefore, honey can alleviate the symptoms of a common cold or flu.

- **Treating dandruff:** The anti-inflammatory properties of honey also help treat seborrheic dermatitis as well as dandruff while also dealing with scalp redness and itchiness.

- **Improving memory:** Honey has also shown to be very effective in preventing cell damage within the brain because of its antioxidants. It also helps your body absorb calcium, which is good for your brain's health.

- **Ideal sugar substitute:** You can use honey in all the places that need sugar because it is a healthier substitute.

- **Prevents acid reflux:** Honey has shown proven capable of lining the walls of the stomach and esophagus, thus reducing the upward flow of undigested food and stomach acid. Therefore, honey can help ward off acid reflux.

On the other hand, beeswax, another hive byproduct, has a multitude of natural benefits. This substitute is usually edible, but most of its benefits are for the skin and hair. Some of these benefits include:

- **Protection from irritants:** Beeswax can act as a protective layer when applied to the skin. It can protect the skin from environmental irritants and extreme weather.

- **Moisturizing components:** You can also use beeswax to lock down moisture, which is good for the skin. It helps keep the skin plump and firm due to its anti-inflammatory properties and anti-allergenic properties. That makes it the perfect ingredient for healing eczema and rosacea skin problems.

- **Promotion of hair growth:** Wax maintains the moisture in your hair and helps soothe the hair from any irritation. It can also reduce hair loss and stimulate hair growth.

These are some of the most common advantages of honey and beeswax due to their beneficial properties. Therefore, honey and beeswax are generally good for your health, and if possible, you can incorporate honey in your food and beauty products. Let's now focus on how to keep your bees in perfect health. When your bees are healthy, you can be sure of a plentiful harvest.

Chapter 8
Healthy Bees and Productive Colony

Every beekeeper dreams of a healthy colony that produces a lot of honey and beeswax. After all, very few things are as frustrating or as disappointing as doing everything right only to lose a colony that ought to be growing.

This chapter will look at what you need to do to assess your colony for any problems and what to do about any problems you find. When your colony is strong and healthy, it has a better chance of surviving diseases, pest infestations, or an upcoming harsh winter.

Therefore, being on the lookout for some of the common signs of a strong and healthy colony will help you spot one that does not meet the description of a healthy and strong colony.

Signs of a Healthy Hive

There are certain things you can check in your colony to know if your bees are healthy. Those things include:

#: *A strong and healthy queen*

The first thing you should check is the health of your queen because it determines whether your colony will grow. The queen is usually the one responsible for reproducing and keeping the population up. She also releases pheromones that tell the other bees she alive, motivating them to keep working on making brood, protecting the hive, and making honey.

That's why you need to check on the queen whenever you inspect. That makes it easier to spot and rectify queen-less hive, which can be dangerous. If you realize your hive has no queen or it is growing at a slow rate, make sure to replace her.

#: *Plenty of honey and pollen stores*

If your hive does not have enough pollen and honey stores, then something is not okay. Pollen stores are usually near the brood to check and see, or you can look out for forager bees that come back to the hive with pollen baskets on their legs.

A plentiful supply means that your colony is healthy, but pollen and honey stores alone cannot guarantee a healthy hive. So monitor that factor together with other factors.

#: *No pests or parasites*

Another sign of a healthy colony is that there should be no pests or parasites. Therefore, you should look for signs of these and other pests, diseases, or parasites during your inspections. And so, when you notice any webs from moths or mites and crawling beetles, you need to take action.

If your colony is healthy and strong, it shouldn't be too much of a struggle to keep pests at bay. One good conductor of a healthy hive is a clean comb. You can address this situation by using pesticides or cleaning your hives.

#: A thriving population

A healthy hive requires thousands of worker bees, and therefore, the more the bees, the healthier the colony. Conversely, a small population would mean fewer workers responsible for caring for the brood and guarding bees.

Thus, pay attention to the traffic going in and out of the hive to monitor your hive population. A colony with a good population will have bees between frames or hanging out on top. Therefore, if you notice that your hive has a small population, there is something wrong, and you need to find a way to increase it.

#: A healthy and regular brood pattern

As much as you might have a strong and healthy queen and workers, you also need to secure the future by ensuring your hive has a healthy brood pattern.

When conducting your regular inspections, you need to make sure your queen is doing her job well by ensuring each cell has an egg. Also, your hive should have a brood pattern that is regular. This essentially means that the comb will have a grouping of solid capped brood cells. If you notice uncapped or holes in the cells, it means the workers have removed the unhealthy larvae.

This means that if this happens, it is likely that there is maybe a problem with pests or diseases. You can also check on the brood themselves because healthy larvae will be pearly white and sit curled in their cell. If you happen to see discolored, malformed, or twisted larvae, your brood is suffering from a disease.

Disease Management and Guidelines for Bees

Besides monitoring your colon's health, you also need to be on the lookout for common issues to determine if your bees are suffering from any pest or disease.

Here are the most common issues that affect bees and how you can manage them.

Tracheal mites

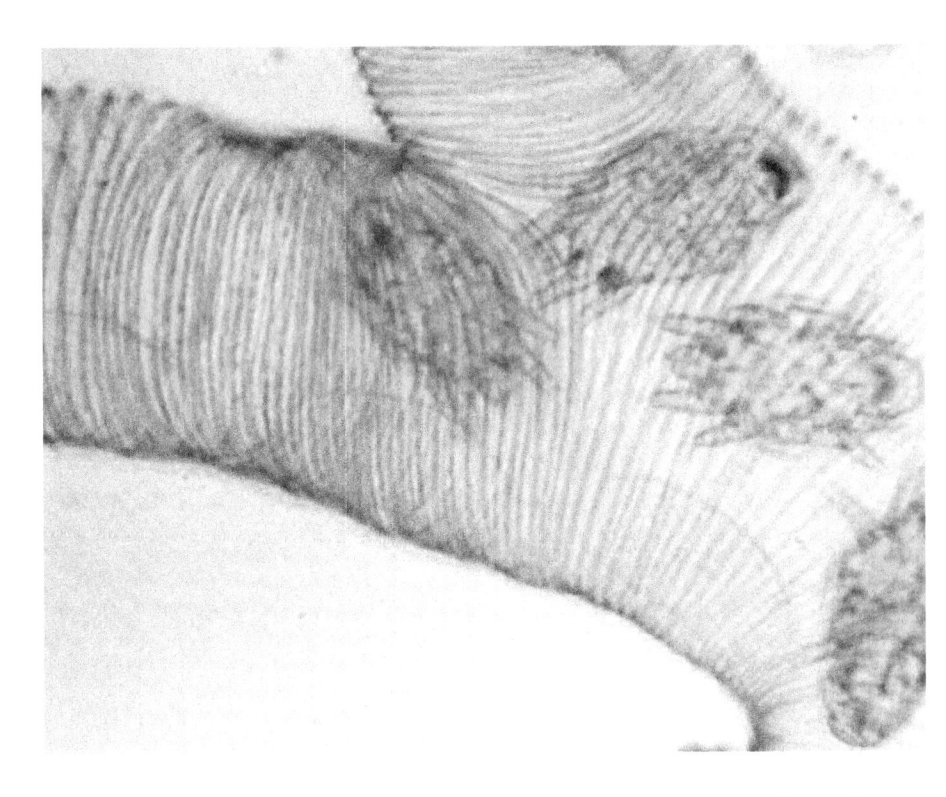

Tracheal mites are internal parasites that live within the trachea or breathing tubes of adult bees. These mites might be in air sacs, head, and abdomen.

This parasitic mite usually manifests itself through disjointed wings, and the bees often crawl on the bottom board often looking morbid. Using a microscope is the most effective way of identifying this infestation.

However, most bees have developed a natural resistance to them. If you happen to notice the signs, measure the infestation levels. If the number of infected workers is 10 percent or higher, you need to take active action.

NOTE: Apply treatment only in the late summer or autumn.

Small hive beetle

This pest first came into the limelight in Florida 1998 in spring. This pest originated in Africa then spread to other parts.

The best way to detect this pest is by the presence of adult beetles and eggs or larvae. Another symptom is the presence of a watery and fermenting honeycomb with small white grubs that seem to be feeding on the wax. Also, the larvae will crawl out of the comb and burrow into the soil.

If adult beetles are present, then tape a ½ a strip of checkmite+ beneath the bottom board in a square of corrugated cardboard.

If the larvae are present and crawling out of the hive, replace the affected combs or burn or freeze them if salvageable. You can also apply Guardstar soil drench around the perimeter of the hive to kill developing pupae.

Sacbrood

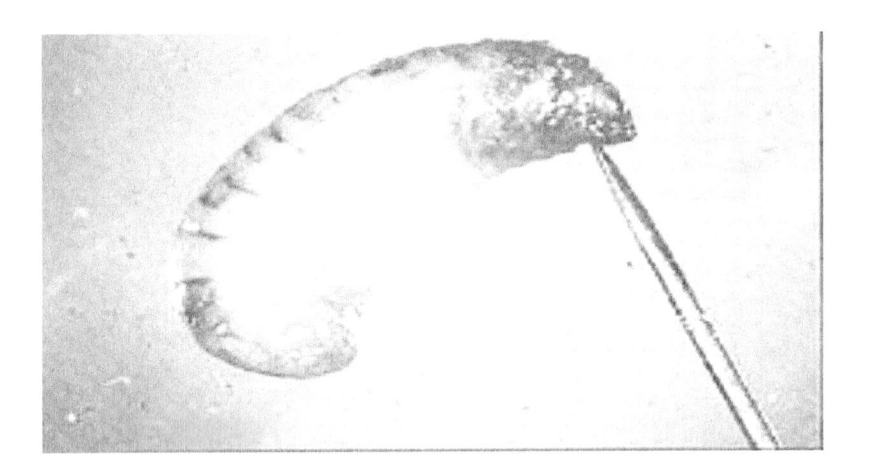

This viral pathogen of bee larvae is responsible for causing the death of larvae. You can notice this disease by dead larvae that appear granular as well as watery with a sac formed by thick skin.

The shape of the head of infected larvae usually lifts its head to the top of the cell such that it resembles the shape of a canoe.

You can easily prevent this disease by maintaining a strong and healthy colony because the disease is stress-caused.

Unfortunately, there are no chemotherapies for reversing/treating sacbrood; requeening might be beneficial.

Chalkbrood

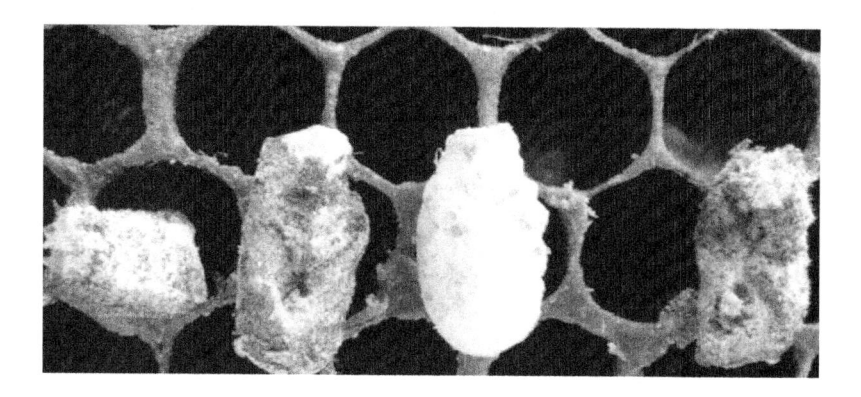

Chalkbrood is a fungal disease normally caused by stress. You can detect this disease by checking for hardened, white, or black organisms that resemble chalk. You can find these organisms located inside or uncapped brood cells, or they may litter the bottom board outside the hive.

These diseases are preventable by maintaining a strong and healthy colony. Also, cold might increase chalkbrood; thus, it is important to ensure a big adult population that keeps the brood nest warm.

Unfortunately, there are no chemotherapies for chalkbrood, but requeening may help the situation.

Wax Moths

These larvae affect the honeycombs of weak hives. You can detect this disease when you observe silk cocoons usually found on the sidebars or topbars of infested hive frames. Also, if you notice large 1.5-inch larvae tunneling through the wax of the combs, then the Wax Moths have infested your hive.

To prevent this disease, you can maintain a strong and healthy colony or cycle the combs through the freezer for 1 to 2 days before storing them.

You can treat this disease by storing unused combs with PDB crystals but never place them on living combs. If by any chance you find a high infestation, then freeze the combs for 1 to 2 days before reusing.

Varroa Mites

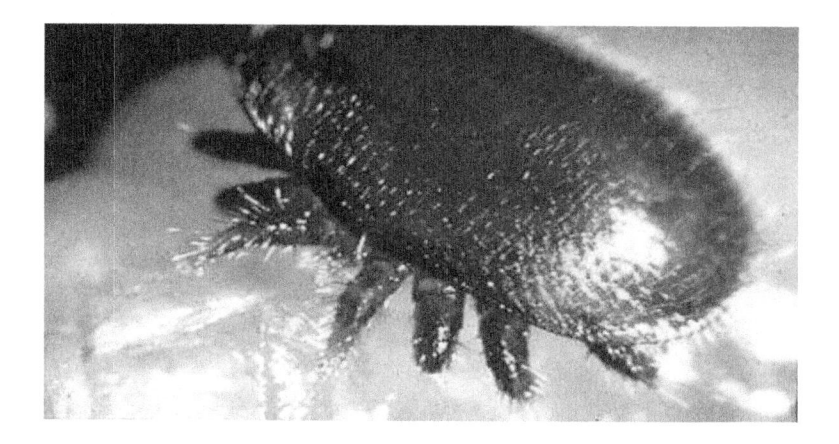

This parasitic mite affects adult bees. You can detect their presence by observing adult bees with a shortened abdomen, deformed legs, and misshapen. Another sign is adult mites on the adult bees or a dramatic decrease in the adult population.

You can detect Varroa mites through sugar shake, sticky board, alcohol wash, and drone brood inspection.

If the varroa mites are equal or more than 2 to 3 mites per 100 adult bees, then use a volatile treatment such as formic acid and thymol. You can only do this in spring.

During summer or late spring, you cannot use these chemicals. Thus, you can only use screen bottom boards.

Try rotating the control measures to minimize the likelihood of mites developing resistance.

American Foulbrood

This spore-forming bacteria causes the brood to look dull-white such that it looks light brown. The signs of this disease include the sealed brood is discolored and sunken, and the brood cells will have brittle, black scales from the dried diseased brood.

You can prevent this disease by keeping your colony strong, replacing combs each year, hygiene stocks, and disinfecting beehives.

You can treat this disease by burning all the frames and euthanizing the bees. Also, you can try scorching or fumigating empty brood boxes, inner cover, bottom boards, and lids.

Nosema

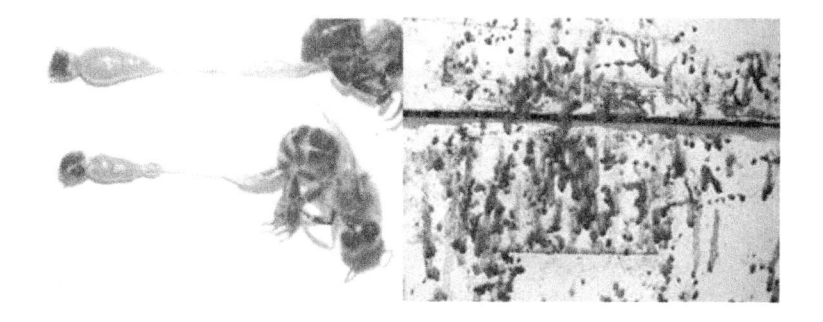

This protozoan causes adult bees to have a distended abdomen and defecate within the hive instead of outside.

Stress is the main cause of this disease, which means that a strong and healthy colony can help prevent this disease. However, unfortunately, you can only know for sure your bees are suffering from Nosema by dissecting their digestive system.

If there are more than one million spores per bee, the best treatment is the Furmadil-B with sugar syrup and feed the bees. You should do this in early spring before the honey season. You cannot use this measure during summer, but you can use it in autumn.

These are some of the most common problems that bees face. If not taken care of, these pests and diseases can destroy your colony, causing many losses. However, if you're keen enough to look out for those symptoms and act as soon as you spot anything, then you'll be good to go.

Bees Absconding

Bee absconding is a term used when a colony of bees leaves their home searching for a new and better habitat. Do not confuse it with swarming. Swarming involves the colony splitting, with one colony staying in the old home while others look for a new home. On the other hand, absconding involves all the bees leaving permanently.

The bees can leave their home for many reasons that make a hive inhabitable. These issues include:

- Too high or low temperatures
- Poor ventilation

- Large animal braids
- A large population
- Inadequate food and water
- Issues with the queen.
- High humidity and poor drainage
- Disease and parasites attack
- Agrochemicals.
- Strong winds
- And much more

As you can see, losing your entire colony is not a risk you can accommodate. The best way to keep this from happening is to address the issues listed above and find ways to prevent incurring losses.

Where to get help

If you happen to encounter problems you can't manage, or you want further help in taking care of your bees, then there are ways you can get help.

First, you can try reaching out to your local beekeepers association if there's one. If not, you can try reaching out to your State's department of agriculture. They will give you all the necessary information you need.

The internet can help you find the nearest vet. Make sure to connect with other beekeepers in your area so that you can find guidance.

Conclusion

Notwithstanding all the beekeeping knowledge you now have, the bulk of the work remains with you. Moreover, your success as a beekeeper is in your hands.

As long as you follow the steps given to you faithfully, the journey towards becoming a seasoned beekeeper will be quite easy and fun.

Here are some highly recommended reads that can help you:

- The Honey Bee by Kristen Hall
- Give Bees A Chance by Bethany Barton
- The Magic School Bus Inside A Beehive by Joanne Cole
- Please Please The Bees by Gerald Kelly.

Here are some of the foundations and organizations supporting bee lovers:

BEES for the World, Germany

http://beesfortheworld.de/

Pollinator partnership Canada, Canada

https://pollinatorpartnership.ca/en

Bees for development, United Kingdom

https://beesfordevelopment.org/

The honeybee conservancy, United States

https://thebeeconservancy.org/

United Nations Development projects, International

http://bees.undp.org/

If you've found this book interesting and informative, don't forget to leave a positive review or feedback.

Thank you for reading, and good luck in becoming an amazing beekeeper!

Printed in Great Britain
by Amazon